1 CORINTHIANS

PRINCIPLES FOR LIVING
IN CHRISTIAN COMMUNITY

Light to My Path Series

Old Testament

Ezra, Nehemiah, and Esther
Job
Isaiah
Jeremiah and Lamentations
Ezekiel
Amos, Obadiah, and Jonah
Micah, Nahum, Habakkuk, and Zephaniah
Haggai, Zechariah, and Malachi

New Testament

John
Acts
Romans
1 Corinthians
2 Corinthians
Philippians and Colossians
James and 1 & 2 Peter
The Epistles of John and Jude

1 Corinthians

Principles for Living in Christian Community

F. Wayne Mac Leod

Authentic

Authentic Media
We welcome your comments and questions.
129 Mobilization Drive, Waynesboro, GA 30830 USA authentic@stl.org
and 9 Holdom Avenue, Bletchley, Milton Keynes, Bucks, MK1 1QR, UK
www.authenticbooks.com

If you would like a copy of our current catalog, contact us at:
1-8MORE-BOOKS
ordersusa@stl.org

1 Corinthians
ISBN: 1-932805-47-8

09 08 07 06 / 6 5 4 3 2 1

Published in 2006 by Authentic Media

Cover design: Paul Lewis
Interior design: Angela Duerksen
Editorial team: Bette Smyth, Betsy Weinrich, Tom Richards

Printed in the United States of America

Contents

Preface

The letter of 1 Corinthians was written to a church that had many struggles. The church at Corinth wrestled with division. Believers sided with their favorite leaders, even questioning the ministry of the apostle Paul himself. Some in the church depended too much on their human wisdom and needed correction. Others were taking fellow believers to court. One man was caught in sexual immorality and the issue had simply been swept under the carpet. Still others were coming to the Lord's Table and getting drunk. Some questioned whether Christ had risen from the dead. And many Corinthians had questions about marriage, idols, spiritual gifts, the role of women in ministry, and the resurrection.

Paul wrote 1 Corinthians to help the believers in Corinth answer questions they had about some practical matters of theology and to deal with behavioral issues in the church that needed correction. In 1 Corinthians Paul lovingly addressed the church of Corinth on these issues. At times he spoke boldly to them. He gave them a series of guidelines for healthy worship and Christian living, answered their questions, and challenged them to learn how to love each other with God's love.

As with all the commentaries in this series, the goal of this book is to walk you systematically through the book of 1 Corinthians. I have written it in such a way that it can be used in your personal quiet time with the Lord. I encourage you to take the time to go through 1 Corinthians using this book as a guide. The goal of this commentary is not to replace the Bible but to complement it and to make it easier to understand. Please read the Bible passage referenced with each chapter. Take the time to consider the questions at the end of each chapter.

The commentaries in this series are being sent to needy pastors and Christian workers around the world. I have been encouraged by letters returning from these servants of God in Africa and Asia telling me how God has used the commentaries in their ministries. Would you take a moment to pray that the Lord would use this particular book to encourage and bless a pastor or Christian worker in Africa or Asia?

May God be pleased to draw you closer to himself through this work.

F. Wayne Mac Leod

1

Introduction

Read 1 Corinthians 1:1–9

This letter was written by the apostle Paul to the believers in Corinth. In Paul's day Corinth was a significant trade city and home of the pagan goddess Aphrodite, goddess of love. Paul spent almost a year and a half ministering in Corinth.

As he began his letter to the Corinthians, Paul reminded them that he was called to be an apostle by the will of God. He placed his credentials before them. He reminded them of his position because it was important that they know he was writing to them from a position of authority. He emphasized his divine authority here because of the nature of the issues that had come up in the church. He wrote as one who has been called and empowered of God. He had a word from the Lord for them. They were to take what he had to say with all seriousness.

The letter also came from Sosthenes. We are not sure about the identity of Sosthenes (verse 1). Many believe him to be a synagogue ruler in Corinth who was converted under Paul's ministry (see Acts 18:17). Sosthenes would have been well known in Corinth and would not need any introduction.

The letter is addressed to "the church of God in Corinth" (verse 2). Notice first that this church belonged to God. The church did not belong to the Corinthians. It was not their invention. Those who belonged to this church belonged to God. Second, the church was comprised of those who had been *sanctified* in Christ Jesus. Sanctified means set apart both in character and in lifestyle for the Lord Jesus and his purposes. Those who belonged to this church of God had set themselves apart for him, and he was shaping them into his character. Third, those in this church were called to be holy. This was their obligation. They were to live as God requires. They were to turn from their old ways to serve and live entirely for the Lord Jesus. Notice that Paul told the Corinthians that this is what God expects of his people everywhere and not just in the city of Corinth. This brings us to the fourth characteristic of this church. It was not just one little assembly of people located on a certain street in Corinth. The church of God is much bigger than that. Everyone who has been set apart by God through the sacrificial death of Christ and called by him to be holy is part of this church. These Corinthians belonged to a universal body of people that would span the globe and stretch throughout time.

In verse 3, Paul offered the Corinthians his blessing: "Grace and peace to you from God our Father and the Lord Jesus Christ." Grace refers to the unmerited favor of the Lord Jesus offered to undeserving sinners. Peace is not an absence of problems but a right relationship with God. This was Paul's desire for the Corinthians. He wanted them to experience the unmerited favor of God and a deep assurance that they were in a right relationship with him.

Paul had a very large heart of compassion. He had never met many of these believers. We will see that some of them had fallen into sin (some even into very deep sin). He still thanked God for them. His heart was filled to overflowing with thanksgiving (verse 4). Despite their sin, Paul knew them to be God's children, and he loved them as such. There is indication in this book that some people in Corinth did not care much for Paul. This did not matter. They belonged to God and because God loved them, Paul loved them too.

Do we have the same attitude as Paul? Let us be honest with ourselves. Some Christians are very hard to love. Paul had the ability, however, to see these individuals as God saw them. Are there believers that you cannot thank God for today? Paul could have held grudges or bitterness in his heart toward certain of these Corinthians, but he refused to fall into this trap. May God give us the grace to follow Paul's example.

Paul began this letter by looking at the positive characteristics of the Corinthian believers. Let's examine each of these characteristics individually.

In Him You Have Been Enriched (verse 5)

The Corinthian believers had been enriched by Christ in every way. This enrichment was in two particular areas. First, they were enriched in their words ("speaking"). In 2 Corinthians 8:7, Paul said that the Corinthians excelled in speech and knowledge. Very obviously, they were not keeping the message of the gospel to themselves. They were spreading this message of Christ to those around them. They spoke the Word of God with boldness. This was a sign of the blessing of God on their lives. God had gifted them with boldness to share his Word.

Second, the Corinthian believers were enriched in knowledge. They did not share Christ out of ignorance. They knew the Scriptures and understood the truth of God. They could share the great doctrines of the church with those around them. They had answers for those who asked them the reason for the hope they had (1 Peter 3:15). God had blessed this church with evangelistic zeal and depth of understanding of the Scriptures.

Our Testimony about Christ Was Confirmed in You (verse 6)

When Paul looked at the way the work of God was progressing in the region of Corinth, he took great comfort in it. What he shared with them about the person and work of Christ when he lived among them was being demonstrated in their lives. They were experiencing the power of the risen Lord in their daily life. While Paul understood that they still had certain problems, no one could deny that Jesus was doing a mighty work through them. They were a testimony to a living and all-powerful Christ.

You Do Not Lack Any Spiritual Gift (verse 7)

The power of the living Christ was evident in the way the Corinthians experienced and used their spiritual gifts. Often we have to encourage people to use the gifts God has given them. This was not the case in Corinth. The Corinthians were known for their spiritual gifts. They used them and experienced the power of God in their midst.

You Eagerly Wait for the Lord Jesus to Be Revealed (verse 7)

Another important characteristic of the Corinthian church was their eager longing for the Lord's return. Paul spent time in this letter answering some questions the Corinthians had about the Lord's return. This was a preoccupation for them in their ministry. They longed for the day when the Lord would return to take them to be with him.

Paul reminded the Corinthians in verse 8 that God would keep them strong to the end, to the day of Christ. He was confident that God was able to perfect this church and make it everything he intended it to be. Although these believers were presently experiencing many trials and difficulties, Paul was still confident that the Lord who called them would not abandon them (verse 9). God had called the Corinthians out of sin and to himself. Now that they belonged to him, he would never abandon them. Even when they fell into unfaithfulness and error, God would remain faithful to them.

For Consideration:

- Is there anyone you have trouble loving and for whom you have a hard time thanking God? Ask God for the grace necessary to thank him for this person today.

- Look at the positive characteristics of the church in Corinth. How does your church measure up to this church? How do you personally measure up?

- Are you facing a trial in your life today? What encouragement do you receive from this passage?

For Prayer:

- Ask God to help you demonstrate the positive character traits of the church in Corinth.

- Thank the Lord that he has promised to complete the work he began in you. Ask him to show you the areas of your life he is working on today.

- Take a moment to consider the people God has placed in your life. Thank the Lord for each of them.

2

Paul, Apollos, Cephas, and Christ

Read 1 Corinthians 1:10–17

We saw in the last meditation that the church in Corinth had many positive characteristics. They were far from perfect, however. Here in this next section, we see that the church suffered from various divisions.

Paul began by appealing for unity. He urged the Corinthians to agree with one another so that there would be no more division among them. Notice in verse 10 that he appealed to them as brothers. He did not place himself above them. By addressing them as brothers, he showed tender affection toward them. And notice that he did so in the name of "our Lord Jesus." He spoke to them on the Lord's behalf and with his authority. He spoke as a brother with the authority of an apostle.

Paul's desire for the believers in Corinth was that they agree with one another and be perfectly united in mind and thought (verse 10). This statement could cause us to wonder if Paul really understood human nature. Is there such a thing as a church where everyone agrees with each other and all are united perfectly in mind and thought? Is Paul expecting something from these believers that was simply not possible? What did he mean by this statement?

In Romans 14, Paul spoke to the Romans about accepting those who were weak in the faith (verse 1). He reminded them that some people considered one day as being more important or sacred than another (verse 5) and concluded by encouraging each believer to live in such a way that they accepted their differences and put no stumbling block in front of each other (verses 19–20). From this we gather that Paul understood that even in the healthiest churches, there would be differences of opinion in minor doctrine and practice.

Paul was addressing a very particular issue in 1 Corinthians. From verse 11 we understand that a piece of information had reached him concerning the church in Corinth. He had heard that there were quarrels among believers in the church. It appears from verse 12 that people were divided over personalities. The Corinthians were forming cliques that identified with the ministry style and personality of certain respected leaders. Some were looking to Paul, others to Apollos or Cephas (the apostle Peter), and still others to Christ. Each group thought itself better than the others.

The body of Christ should not be divided (verse 13). Although each of the human leaders had different gifts and ministry focus, the church should stay united under Christ alone. Paul, for example, was a very strong missionary leader. Acts 18:24 tells us that Apollos was a very knowledgeable man in the Scriptures. Peter was an apostle to the Jews. While these various focuses were meant to give the body a fuller ministry, the believers in Corinth were quarrelling over them. Satan was successful in using the strengths of these leaders to divide the church. We need to see how subtle the enemy is in his attacks. He can use our strengths to accomplish his diabolic purposes.

Satan has succeeded in dividing the church of our day in a similar way. Some believers feel the need for extensive effort in local evangelism. Others see the need to reach out in missions. Some prefer a strong emphasis on the teaching of the Word while others prefer to focus on worship or fellowship. Sometimes the local church develops cliques. Groups of people tend to gravitate toward each other. We associate with those with whom we are most comfortable. In the larger body of Christ, I have met believers who were bowing the knee to their church tradition and doctrine. Others seem to worship their church building or denomination. The church in Corinth was not the only church to struggle with problems such as these. They are very real in our day as well.

Paul was addressing this situation when he told the church in Corinth that they needed to be of one mind and thought and agree with one another. They needed to stop allowing these issues to divide them. They needed to put aside their petty preferences and come together on the issues that really mattered. "Is Christ divided?" asked Paul (verse 13). Did Paul die on the cross for your sins? Were you baptized in the name of Paul? The Corinthians could not miss Paul's point. It would be blasphemous to think that Paul was crucified for them. Their worship and devotion were to be toward the Lord Jesus alone. The enemy had been successful in diverting their attention from Christ to their leaders.

Paul reminded the Corinthians that he had not baptized any of them (except Crispus, Gaius, and Stephanas). The Corinthians were not to be followers of Paul but of the Lord Jesus. How easy it is as leaders to seek followers. We who are in leadership know the temptation to seek the adoration and praise of those we work among. Paul refused to fall into this trap. He was not interested in the praise and adoration of people. His desire was that the Lord Jesus be lifted up. God had not sent him to baptize and gain a following of believers for himself. He did not come to preach his own wisdom and gain support for his own theological views. There was no power in this sort of faith (verse 17).

Paul issued a strong exhortation to unity by warning the Corinthians about becoming followers of human leaders and

perspective of the world of Paul's day, that the preaching of the glories of the cross would not have been understood.

On the other hand, from the perspective of the believer, the cross was a very different thing indeed. The cross did not represent defeat and death. It represented life, victory, and hope. It was there on the cross that their sins were forgiven. The cross was not just the final humiliation of Jesus but his ultimate victory. The cross represented power over death, sin, and Satan.

According to Paul, the wisdom of this world could not compare to the power of the cross. By our earthly wisdom, we can have everything this world has to offer. By means of worldly wisdom, we can amass wealth, prestige, and influence. No amount of worldly wisdom, however, can forgive our sins. No amount of worldly wisdom can keep a sinner from an eternity of hell. The cross alone can rescue us from the jaws of Satan and set us free.

Paul reminded the Corinthians that God would destroy the wisdom of the wise (verse 19). "Where is the wise man?" asked Paul in verse 20. Where has all this worldly wisdom led us? By worldly wisdom we have made our lives more convenient. We have managed to prolong life by our medical advances and have found cures for diseases once thought incurable. We have simplified communications and are now able to travel easily from one part of this earth to another. Have all these advances drawn us any closer to God? Has it prepared us any better to face God on the day of judgment? What do we really gain if we have all the comforts and luxuries of this life but spend an eternity separated from God?

The Jews of Paul's day were looking for a miraculous sign (verse 22). The Greeks were looking for great wisdom. What Paul had to offer, however, was the simple message of Christ crucified (verse 23). The Jews rejected the cross. It was a stumbling block for them. To the Jewish mind, the cross could not offer any hope because Jesus did not save himself from death. A crucified Messiah was the end of hope. It was an offence to them who believed that the blessings of God would rest on

Messiah. The Gentiles did not accept the message of the cross because it was not rational enough for them. The cross did not make worldly sense to the Greek mind, and so it was rejected. To those who believed and accepted the cross, however, they found it to be the power and wisdom of God for salvation (verse 24).

Even in our day, many people fall into one of these categories. We have met people who could not accept the message of the cross because they were waiting for a thunderbolt from heaven. Unless they have a "Damascus Road" experience like Paul (see Acts 9), they cannot accept the message of the gospel. Like the Jews of Jesus' day, they are looking for a great sign from heaven before turning to God.

On the other hand, there are those who cannot accept the message of the cross because it is not rational enough for them. They cannot understand how the death of Christ could give them eternal life. Until they understand this, they are not going to accept it. They dismiss the message of the cross as foolishness. They see it as being only for the superstitious or weak minded. What they fail to understand is that the foolishness of God is much wiser than the greatest human wisdom (verse 24). God's wisdom does not conform to our view of wisdom. But when God calls Jews and Gentiles to salvation, they come to understand that Christ, in his work on the cross, is the ultimate power and wisdom.

Paul turned his attention to the Corinthians in verse 26. For the most part, they were a very simple people. There were not many in the church of Corinth who were considered by the world's standard to be wise and influential. In the eyes of the world, they were insignificant. God, however, took these simple people and did something tremendous in them. He made them his children and inheritors of his great kingdom through the simple message of the cross. None could say, "God saved me from an eternity in hell, because I was rich and influential." There was nothing in them that would have drawn the attention of God. They were not saved by means of human wisdom but through the simple message of the cross.

It was in their weakness that the Lord Jesus came to them. Because of the cross, these Corinthian believers put to shame the wisest people on the earth. The Spirit of God's Son lived in them. They were righteous before God (verse 30). They were a holy people, separated for God. They had been rescued from the enemy at the cost of Jesus' life on the cross. No human wisdom could have brought them to this point. The cross of Christ alone brought this victory.

Paul challenged the Corinthians to put aside their differences and unite under the central theme of the cross of Christ. It was here that they were powerful. It was here that they were united. Though they were insignificant in the eyes of the world, united under the cross they were powerful. When seen in this light, their boasting about being of Paul, or Apollos, or Cephas was foolish. None could claim to be better than another simply for following a certain spiritual leader. Any boasting they did could not be in human wisdom or methods. They could only boast in the person and work of the Lord Jesus on the cross.

I suspect that this principle applies to us equally today. Can we consider ourselves better than our brother or sister in Christ because we belong to a certain church or have a certain doctrine and practice? Are we not, like our brothers and sisters, fully dependent on the cross for everything? All boasting must be in the cross.

For Consideration:

- What is it that keeps your unbelieving friends from the Lord? What do we learn about this from this passage?

- Do you think that there are times when believers are ashamed of the cross because it does not measure up to the wisdom of this world?

- What are some of the things we tend to boast about as believers? Are any of these things truly legitimate? What should be our only boast?

- What is the source of our unity as believers, according to the apostle Paul?

For Prayer:

- Take a moment to pray that God would reach down to your unbelieving friends and show them the power of the cross.

- Have you been guilty of criticizing or looking down on other believers because they do not do things like you? Ask God to forgive you for this.

- Ask God to give you a deeper love for his people, regardless of their doctrinal or denominational flavor.

4

Knowing Christ Crucified

Read 1 Corinthians 2:1–5

In chapter 1, Paul had spoken to the Corinthians about the dangers of depending on human wisdom. He had reminded them that it was not because of their wealth and intelligence that they had been saved from the wrath to come. They were a simple people with a simple message. Their power was not in their own abilities but in the cross of Christ. Next, the apostle showed them how this principle worked itself out in his own personal ministry among them.

In verse 1, Paul reminded the Corinthians that when he came to minister among them, he did not come with great eloquence and human wisdom. It should be understood here that, of all the apostles, the apostle Paul was probably the best educated and most eloquent. A quick look at the New Testament will show you that he wrote the vast majority of the books. Paul had a brilliant mind, but he realized that his great learning was not what was necessary for the ministry in Corinth. When he went to Corinth, he knew that if the gospel message was going to be effective, it would not be because of his wisdom and ability. He knew that he would fail if his ministry was founded on human wisdom and eloquence. Instead, he resolved that, in his ministry in Corinth, he would know only one thing—Christ crucified (verse 2). This merits careful consideration.

For Paul, knowing Christ crucified meant two things. First, it meant that the cross of Christ was the central focus of his preaching and teaching. If there was one thing that he wanted the Corinthians to hear from him, it was the gospel message of Christ. He reminded the Corinthians in verse 4 that his preaching was not filled with human wisdom and persuasive words. His preaching focused on one thing and one thing only—the cross of Christ.

Second, knowing Christ crucified meant that Paul chose to depend on the power of the cross to minister to the Corinthians instead of depending on his own human wisdom. This is what he told the Corinthians in verse 4. He reminded them that his message was not in human wisdom but in Spirit and power. The cross of Christ represented power for Paul. In chapter 1, we read that the message of the cross was the power of God for salvation (1:18).

How often have we been distracted from this vital truth? What is it that is going to convince the world of its need of Christ? We have been taught that success in evangelism depends on our using the right method. How many times have we shared the gospel believing that if only we were able to word things properly, we would be able to win others to the Lord? Where is the power of God in this? Are we not depending on our techniques and worldly wisdom to win the world to Christ? Paul is telling us here that the power to win the world to Christ is the cross itself. The simple presentation of the cross alone is sufficient to save. We do not have to be well educated. We do not have to have an answer for every objection. We simply have to present the message of Christ crucified. This is what God will use to win souls to himself. Even the simplest person can be a powerful witness for the Lord.

Paul told the Corinthians that he purposefully chose to

minister to them in this manner so that their faith would rest not on human wisdom but on God's power (verse 5). It would have been easy for Paul to gain followers for himself. It was more important for him, however, that people see the power of Christ in him than to see his knowledge and eloquence. He wanted his life and message to be so filled with Christ and his power so that people had no alternative but to recognize that the crucified Christ was living and working through him. The result would be that they would be attracted to Christ and not to Paul. What do people see in your life?

There is one more thing we need to mention from this passage. Notice in verse 3 that Paul told the Corinthians that he came to them in weakness, fear, and trembling. It is hard to imagine the great apostle Paul shaking in his boots as he went to Corinth to minister. We often picture the apostle Paul as a man of tremendous confidence and spiritual ability. Paul's confidence, however, was not in himself but in the Lord.

When he was an unbeliever, Paul had great confidence in his natural ability. He showed no lack of confidence when he went to the chief priest for permission to lead in an assault against the church. Now that he was a believer, however, all confidence in his natural ability was gone. He knew that as he ministered in Corinth, the sure way to fail was to lean on this natural talent and ability. He trembled because he knew his inability to reach the city of Corinth in his natural strength and eloquence. He went to Corinth emptied of human pride but trusting in the power of the Lord. That can be a scary thing. It is relatively easy to live in our own strength and planning. It is not so easy to live not knowing where God is going to lead us or where our next meal is going to come from. Paul knew his strength was insufficient for the task. He did not have confidence in himself. I suppose this is where each of us really should be in our ministry. God would prove to be faithful to Paul and use him mightily in Corinth. He can do the same for you if you trust in him and the power of his cross.

For Consideration:

- Take a moment to consider the last time you spoke to someone about the Lord. Were you depending on the Lord or on your own ability to convince them?

- How much of Christ do people see in your service and life?

- What encouragement do you take from this section? Who are the people that God chooses to use to minister in his name?

- What are your fears in ministry? What makes you hold back in service for the Lord? What encouragement do you receive from the fact that Paul trembled as he went to Corinth?

For Prayer:

- Have you found yourself depending on your own ability as you presented Christ to those around you? Ask God to forgive you and help you to walk in his enabling.

- Pray that Christ's power and life would be seen in you.

- Ask God to enable you to be bold in ministry despite your fears and trembling.

5

The Wisdom of the Spirit

Read 1 Corinthians 2:6–16

P aul reminded the Corinthians that the message he preached to them was not in words of human wisdom. That is not to say that the apostle was preaching foolishness to them. On the contrary, he was preaching great wisdom. This wisdom, however, was not the wisdom of this world, which would eventually come to nothing. All that we have achieved in technology and medical advances will amount to nothing in the day of judgment. The apostle Peter reminds us that there is a day coming when the earth as we know it will be burned up and destroyed (2 Peter 3:10).

Paul was not interested in preaching worldly wisdom. The wisdom that Paul preached was a "secret" or mysterious wisdom. This wisdom had existed before time began but had been previously hidden from the world (verse 7). The rulers of Paul's age did not understand this wisdom. If they had understood it, they would not have crucified the Lord Jesus. This leads us to understand that the wisdom that Paul spoke about here was the person and work of the Lord Jesus.

In the gospel of John, the apostle John spoke of Jesus as the "Word" or wisdom of God (John 1:14). Jesus represented the plan of God for the salvation of humanity. In him we find the reason for our existence. How many wise people have sought to understand the purpose and meaning of life? Only in Christ can we know the answers. In him and his work is the great wisdom of God.

There is a tremendous promise for those to whom this wisdom is revealed. Paul reminds us that no eye has ever seen the things that God has planned for those who love him (verse 9). No ear has ever heard the glories that God has in store for those who accept this wisdom. Our minds are not big enough to comprehend the great purpose of God in the person of Christ. Men and women in their worldly wisdom have made life more comfortable and pleasant. Life expectancy has been lengthened. We have cured diseases thought to be fatal. These achievements, however, pale into insignificance when compared to what God has in store for those who love him.

Verse 10 tells us that it is the ministry of the Holy Spirit of God to reveal the profound truths of God to believers. Just as we need our own human spirit to understand worldly wisdom so we need God's Spirit to understand the spiritual wisdom. Without God's Spirit in us, we would never be able to understand or communicate Christ's work of redemption (verse 13). Unbelievers, who lack the supernatural life and wisdom of the Holy Spirit, cannot receive the things of God because these truths are spiritually discerned (verse 14).

Maybe you can identify with this personally. How many times did you sit under the preaching of the gospel? How many times did you hear that the Lord Jesus died for your sins and that if you accepted him into your heart, you could become a child of God? You heard the words, but they did not make sense to you. You were trying to understand without having the capacity to process spiritual thought.

This is what Paul was telling the Corinthians in verse 14. He made it clear that people without the Spirit do not accept the things that come from the Spirit; spiritual things are foolishness to them. Only those who have the Spirit of God can understand the wisdom of God. The message that Paul spoke was a spiritual message. His wisdom could not be found in books written by worldly wise people of his day. His message was from the Spirit of God. He conveyed spiritual wisdom in words given to him by the Holy Spirit, and only those to whom the Spirit revealed this truth could understand it.

While a man or woman without the Spirit could not understand the things that Paul spoke, a spiritual person (who has the Spirit of God) would be able to make judgments about these spiritual matters (verse 15). In other words, spiritual people are able to discuss and consider the things of God because the Holy Spirit, living in them, gives them understanding.

Paul went on to say that the spiritual person "is not subject to any man's judgment" (verse 15). This has caused some difficulty for commentators. Paul meant that unbelievers, who have only a natural understanding of the world, cannot correctly evaluate believers, who have a supernatural understanding of life. Believers will be misunderstood by the world, but ultimately they answer only to God. Because we, as believers, are indwelled by the Spirit of God, we are allowed to know the thoughts of our Lord (verse 16). We are better able than unbelievers to understand situations and make godly decisions, because we are allowed to perceive the world through the eyes of Christ.

All around us, people are perishing in their sins because they do not understand the wisdom of God for salvation. But we have been given the mind of Christ to understand our sin and to believe on the Lord Jesus for forgiveness. How we need to thank the Lord for giving us this understanding.

Knowing that unbelievers cannot understand the things of God should help us to in our presentation of the gospel. What unbelievers need is not another finely polished presentation but the ministry of the Holy Spirit in their lives. This ought to drive us to our knees to seek God on their behalf. We are communicating to people who do not have the capacity to comprehend what we are presenting to them. How important it is that we work in partnership with the Spirit of God. While he uses us in the presentation of the gospel, ultimately he must give the understanding. What a privilege we have to be partners with God in reaching out to this world. What a privilege it is to have our minds opened to understand the deep truths of God.

For Consideration:

- Can you recall the day that you came to understand the message of the gospel for the first time? Can you relate to what Paul is saying here in this passage about being given the mind of God?

- How important is it to have all the right words in our presentation of the gospel? What role do we play in the conversion of a soul to Christ? What role does the Spirit of God play?

- Do you have the mind of Christ? What is the difference between the mind of Christ and the wisdom of this world?

For Prayer:

- Take a moment to pray for an unbeliever in your neighborhood. Ask God to give this person an understanding of the gospel.

- Have you ever found yourself running ahead of God in the presentation of the gospel, believing that you could win the lost to Christ by your own persuasive words? Ask God to forgive you and help you to recognize the role of his Spirit in winning the lost.

- Thank the Lord for how he has opened your mind to spiritual matters.

6

Division in the Corinthian Church

Read 1 Corinthians 3

I n the last meditation, Paul made a distinction between the spiritual person who has the Spirit of God and the worldly person who does not. Here in this chapter, he reminded the Corinthians that the distinction between the spiritual and the worldly person is not always as clear as it ought to be. Although spiritual people have the capacity to live according to God's wisdom, they do not always do so. Often they live and think like the worldly person. Paul told the Corinthians that they were not viewing the world from the spiritual point of view.

Notice in verse 1 that Paul spoke to the Corinthians as "brothers." The term would indicate that he believed them to be God's children. They had accepted the Lord and were part of God's family. Notice, however, that though they were his brothers in the faith, Paul could not address them as "spiritual." While they belonged to the Lord Jesus, they had chosen to live according to the standards and wisdom of the world. What a tragedy this was. They were mere babes in Christ. They had never matured in their faith. Their faith was not being demonstrated in their lives.

Paul could not give them solid food—the deeper truths of God (verse 2). They were still in need of milk in their walk with the Lord. They had been Christians long enough to have demonstrated very real changes in their lives, but this had not happened. Paul told the Corinthians that they were still worldly in their understanding (verse 3).

It is important that we note here that Paul was expecting progress in the Corinthian's walk with the Lord. Has there been progress in your spiritual life? Are you closer to the Lord this year than you were last year? This growth should be seen at every level of your Christian experience. Sometimes we see tremendous growth in the first few years of our relationship with the Lord, and then it seems to fade away. Even the believer who has known the Lord for fifty years needs to continue to mature in godly living. We will never exhaust our understanding of God and his grace. There will always be sins to overcome and new heights of empowerment in our service for Christ. Growth ought to be the normal experience for us.

The Corinthians had never really progressed in their walk with the Lord. One of the evidences of this could be seen in their jealousy and quarrelling. As a church, they were caught up in minor differences. Some people followed Paul; others preferred Apollos. These differences were causing division in the church of Corinth. The mere fact that they had this fragmentation proved that they were not growing in their faith. Instead, they were thinking and behaving as "mere men" (verse 3). That is to say, they were not living any differently than unbelievers.

Paul then showed them in verses 5–6 that both he and Apollos were ministers together in the cause of Christ. God had given to Paul and Apollos different functions in the body of Christ. Paul was the one who planted the seed of truth, and Apollos was the one who watered it. Both of these men were dependent on God to cause the seed to grow and produce fruit in the lives of the Corinthians. Both Paul and Apollos had one goal: they wanted to see the fruit of Christ in the lives of the Corinthians. Paul was demonstrating that it was immature to think that one ministry was more important than another, because God was controlling the process and using different people in different ways.

Paul recognized his role in the life of the Corinthian church. In verse 10 he began using the imagery of constructing a building and said that he had laid the foundation of the church in Corinth. God had used Paul to preach the gospel and establish a new church (see Romans 15:20). Then it was the responsibility of someone else to construct the rest of the building on that foundation. Apollos had done this by teaching the Word of God among them.

Paul reminded the Corinthians that each of them also had the responsibility to continue to build on that foundation, which was the person and work of the Lord Jesus (verse 11). Each of them was in the process of building the church of Christ. As believers, they had a choice of materials to use. They could build wisely by using the best of materials—gold, silver, and costly stones—or they could build unwisely by using wood, hay, and straw (verse 12). Through faithful ministry they could build a solid local church that would stand the test of the flames of God's assessment (verse 13). On the other hand, they could be unfaithful and build their local assembly of wood, hay, and straw. This poorer construction would not stand the test of flames. The day of judgment would bring all these things to light (see 2 Corinthians 5:10). On that day the quality of each person's work for the church of Christ would be revealed.

Paul reminded the Corinthians in verse 15 that he was not speaking about their salvation when he spoke about building on the foundation. That salvation was secure the moment they accepted the Lord as their Savior. The person who built with wood, hay, and straw would suffer tremendous loss on the day of judgment but still be saved "as one escaping through the flames" (verse 15).

Let us examine what Paul was saying here. Paul was telling the Corinthian believers that because their lives were established on the foundation of Christ, they were to do their utmost to build a local church and personal lives that would honor their Lord. They were to serve one another using spiritual wisdom not worldly wisdom.

The way we live our lives here below will be brought to light in the day of judgment. The Bible speaks of rewards for earthly service (Matthew 5:12; 6:1). There are believers who serve the Lord with wood, hay and straw. These believers live and think like unbelievers. Paul reminded the Corinthians that this type of believer would suffer the loss of rewards in heaven. Standing before the Lord their God, they would have nothing to offer him. They had wasted their resources and energy and had proven to be unfaithful servants. God would still love them and accept them as his children, but they would not receive the commendation of their Heavenly Father for their efforts.

As believers, we are temples of God. God's Spirit lives in us (see verse 16). As long as we are here on earth, we are constructing our temples. As God's holy temples, our lives are sacred. We need to be careful not to allow into these temples anything that would bring dishonor to the Lord God who lives in our hearts. It is a serious thing to defile the temple of God. Paul warned the Corinthians that if they defiled their temples, God would destroy them (verse 17). The Corinthians had been guilty of allowing jealousy, quarrels, and division to enter their temples. They would answer to God for this.

What are you building your temple with today? Are you building with blocks of jealousy, bitterness, and division? What adornments can be found on the inside of your temple? What are you allowing your eyes to see? What pictures have you hung up on the wall of your mind? What thoughts are being played through the speakers of your heart?

Paul challenged the Corinthians not to deceive themselves (verse 18). They thought that they were wise. They believed that things were all right between themselves and God, but they were only deceiving themselves. Things were not all right. The Corinthian believers needed to be awakened to the reality of what was taking place in their lives. They were trying to function with worldly wisdom. They were being caught up in worldly ways. They were boasting in men (verse 21). They were lifting up ministry styles and personality traits when they had things of far greater significance to boast about.

Paul reminded them in verse 22 of the blessing that was theirs in Christ. They had wonderful servants of God who had shared his love with them (Cephas, Paul, and Apollos). Beyond this, the world itself was a gift of God to them. Their lives and deaths were in his hands. Their present blessings and their future hope were all gifts from a gracious God to them. They belonged to Christ. He had chosen them and saved them from an eternity of hell and suffering. In light of the wonderful blessings of God, their petty divisions were irrelevant.

As believers, we can still live worldly lives. This is what was happening in the church of Corinth. The believers there were being caught up in petty divisions. The enemy had succeeded in getting their attention off Christ and onto themselves. The result was that they were no longer growing in their faith. Instead, they began to place blocks of jealousy and division on the solid foundation of Christ.

What a challenge this chapter is to us as believers today. As you look at the temple you have been building, what sort of blocks do you find? Perhaps scattered among the blocks of gold, silver, and precious stone can be seen blocks of wood, hay, and straw. These inferior blocks need to be pulled out and replaced with blocks that bring honor to the name of the Lord Jesus.

There are two types of believers. There are those who are spiritual and those who are worldly. Both of them have the same foundation. The difference is the type of material they are building their lives with. The Corinthians had been building with wood, hay, and straw. What are you building with?

For Consideration:

- Has this meditation drawn your attention to some blocks in your life that need to be dealt with? What are those blocks?

- We have seen two types of believers in this chapter. What type of believer are you? What evidence is there of this in your life?

- What evidence of growth do you find in your spiritual walk?

For Prayer:

- Ask God to help you to deal with the blocks in your life that do not bring honor to him.

- Do you know fellow believers who have not been able to grow in their spiritual life because of certain blockages in their lives? Take a moment to pray for them now.

- Thank God for the sure foundation he has given us on which we can build our lives.

7

Called into Question

Read 1 Corinthians 4:1–5

As we have already seen, one of the problems in the Corinthian church was that the church members had become followers of their human leaders. Some had sided with Paul and others with Apollos. In the last meditation, Paul reminded the Corinthians of the foolishness of this divisive attitude that caused Paul some difficulty as he sought to minister among them.

Have you ever had someone call your ministry into question or compare your ministry with someone else's? Paul knew what it was like to be discounted in his ministry. The Lord Jesus himself was not always appreciated. He knew what it was like to have people question his authority. If you are in ministry, you too, sooner or later, will have to face the same opposition. How do we deal with this sort of opposition to our ministries? A look at how the apostle Paul dealt with this should help us in our own times of trial.

He Had a Clear Understanding of His Calling (verse 1)

Probably one of the single most important things we can do as we face opposition and questions about our ministry is to be sure of our calling. If I depended on what others thought of my ministry, there would have been many times when I would have given up. While there have been many difficulties, I have never been able to get beyond the fact that the Lord Jesus one day made it clear that he wanted me in full-time ministry. There have been times in my life when I considered another type of work, but each time the Lord brought me back to his original call. That sense of calling has sustained me through many difficulties.

The apostle Paul had a clear understanding of his call. He understood himself to be a servant to whom Christ had entrusted the "secret things of God" (verse 1). The word *entrust* here is important. God had given him a responsibility. God had trusted him with a message for his people, and Paul knew that he was under obligation to God to share that message. Paul knew that he needed to be faithful no matter what others said about him. Paul was able to face those who questioned him and his ministry because he had a clear understanding of God's call on his life.

He Committed Himself to Being Faithful to His Calling (verse 2)

Having confirmed in his mind what the call of God was for his life, Paul then committed himself to obey that call. The Lord God had given him a trust, and he knew he had to be faithful to that trust.

We can be sure that the enemy will do his best to keep us from being faithful to the trust God has given us. I have probably experienced more frustration in the area of my giftedness than any other area of ministry. Satan has used the reactions of people to discourage me. Sometimes I have questioned my gifting. I have at times gone back to the Lord and asked him if I should continue in this particular ministry.

When challenged in his ministry, the apostle Paul returned to his calling. He also realized that when God entrusted a charge to someone, he expected that individual to prove faithful to that charge. This was Paul's commitment. He made a commitment to his calling and nothing would keep him from faithfulness.

He Refused to Allow Himself to Be Judged by Anyone (verse 3)

Having clarified his calling and commitment to be faithful to that calling, Paul then told the Corinthians that he would not allow himself to be judged by any human court. "I care very little if I am judged by any human court," he told them. Paul told the Corinthians that his commitment was not to please people but God who called him. Paul did not care if he was judged by people. What individuals said about his ministry was not as important as what the Lord said. He chose to be faithful to God rather than humans.

I have found this to be a lot easier to say than to practice. How often I have become fixated on what others thought about my ministry? I want to be liked. I feel the need for appreciation and support, and I often look to people to give me this support and encouragement. The danger in this is becoming a people-pleaser.

Throughout the Scriptures we see God calling his servants to stand against the current. When I made my wedding vows to my wife, I committed myself to being faithful to her alone for the rest of my life. In making those vows, I knew that no one else was to stand between us. Similarly, in accepting his call from the Lord, the apostle Paul made a commitment. His commitment was to the Lord his God. What others said really did not matter. He would not allow others to distract him from his calling. It was not important that people liked him and his message.

Joseph made an enemy of Potiphar's wife when he refused to sleep with her (Genesis 39). Though she pleaded with him day after day, he refused to defile himself. Daniel too made many enemies when he refused to stop praying to his God (Daniel 6). This even resulted in him being thrown into the lion's den. Faithfulness to the call of God in our lives will sometimes lead us to the path of rejection and scorn. Paul had eyes and ears for no one else. His commitment was to please God. It did not matter what others said.

He Refused Even to Judge Himself (verse 3)

Notice here that Paul not only refused to allow others to judge him in the matter of God's calling in his life, but he also refused to judge himself. Paul has just told us that he refused to listen to those who called into question what he knew to be the clear direction of God for his life. In the same way, Paul refused to allow his own doubts and questions to distract him from that clear calling of God.

Sometimes we are our own worst enemy. How many times have we questioned our own abilities and gifting? The enemy often plagues us with doubt about our own calling and ability. How many times have I gone to God with serious doubts created by my own mind about whether I was the person for the task God had called me to do? How many times would I have left the ministry if I had been listening to my own feelings and doubts? Many people in Scripture seemed to struggle in the same way. Moses called his own ministry into question when he told God that he was not an able speaker (Exodus 4:10–13). Jeremiah, in the face of much opposition, wondered if it would not have been better for him to simply be quiet and not speak anymore (Jeremiah 20:9). I wonder if Peter, after denying the Lord three times, called his own ministry as a disciple into question.

Paul realized that the call of God in his life transcended even his own feelings and doubts. Paul refused to allow himself the privilege of calling his own ministry into question. He would not question what God had made clear to him.

He Maintained a Clear Conscience (verse 4)

In face of opposition to his ministry, Paul sought to maintain a clear conscience. Paul maintained a clear conscience by refusing to allow others to distract him from his God-given calling. He maintained a clear conscience by refusing to allow his own personal doubts to distract him. Paul reminded the

Corinthians that this did not mean he was perfect. He knew that in his ministry he made mistakes. Despite these shortcomings, however, he knew he was where God wanted him to be. In this he had a clear conscience. He chose to live in obedience to God and be faithful to what God had clearly laid out for him. What others said did not matter.

He Waited for the Lord to Bring to Light the Motives of the Heart (verse 5)
Notice finally that Paul committed all judgment to the Lord Jesus. He knew that the only judgment concerning his ministry that mattered was the judgment of the Lord. In his ministry his motivations and methods were often called into question. Paul felt no need to prove what his motives were to others. He committed these matters to the Lord. The day was coming when the Lord would judge the motives of his heart. Until that time, Paul persevered in what he knew was the call of God in his life.

How often has the enemy succeeded in distracting us by causing us to focus on what others were saying about us? Paul refused to be distracted by these things. He committed all judgment to the Lord and continued with his ministry. May God give us the grace to do the same.

For Consideration:

• What has God entrusted to you? What are your gifts? What ministries has he clearly given you?

• Have you been faithful to the ministry God has given you?

• Have you ever found yourself distracted in ministry because of what others were saying about you? What challenge do you receive from this passage?

For Prayer:

• Thank God for the gifts and calling he has given you.

- If you are not sure of what God's ministry is for you, take a moment to ask him to give you a clear sense of his gifting and calling.

- Ask God to open doors of opportunity for you to exercise his calling on your life. Ask him to help you to be faithful to that calling.

8

Comfortable Christianity

Read 1 Corinthians 4:6–21

Paul had been speaking to the Corinthians about the divisions in their midst. They had been elevating one teacher above another in their assembly. This disunity was rooted in petty jealousies. Paul addressed this spirit of pride and envy in this passage.

Paul began in verse 6 by telling the Corinthians that they should not go beyond what was written. By taking pride in one person over another, they were going beyond the bounds of how God sees things. The clear teaching of the Word of God is that everything we have we have received from the hands of God (verse 7). We have nothing to boast of in ourselves or in our human leaders. What have we ever done that we did not owe to God? As great as the apostle Paul was, he knew that everything he accomplished was a result of God's grace and power. Paul knew that he was no different from any other servant of God. All his efforts for the gospel were the result of the work of an almighty God in his life. His life, his ministry, and everything he was or ever could be, he received as an unmerited gift from the hand of a sovereign God. If there were to be any boasting, it would have to be in the Lord and what he could accomplish through the life of an undeserving sinner.

The Corinthians did not understand this concept. In their pride, many of them believed that they had achieved spiritual maturity. They saw themselves as being spiritually rich (verse 8). They felt that they were ruling like spiritual kings in their city. Paul saw things differently. "I wish you really had become kings," he said.

While the Corinthians lived comfortably in their church, arguing about which spiritual leader they should follow, the apostles were on display before the world like men condemned to die. The Corinthians saw themselves as kings, while Paul saw himself as a criminal in the arena (verse 9). In contrast to the easy and comfortable lives of the Corinthians, the apostles were suffering the insults and jeers of the crowd looking for their death. In the eyes of the world, the apostles were considered fools.

In their community the Corinthians had maintained an air of respectability. The apostles, on the other hand, were seen by the world as weak and insignificant. Paul had often been insulted and mocked. Wherever he went he suffered dishonor. He knew what it was like to go hungry and thirsty. Unlike the Corinthians, the apostles did not wear the latest fashions. They lived in rags and had nowhere to call home (verse 11). They had to work hard to find enough money to pay for their own ministries. When people cursed them, they blessed them in return. When they were slandered, they responded with words of kindness. People saw them as the "scum" and "refuse" of the earth (verse 13). This was in direct contrast to the how the Corinthians saw themselves—as kings.

The Corinthians had become comfortable in their Christian lifestyle. They enjoyed a respectable reputation in the community. They lived like kings. They were happy with where they were in their spiritual pilgrimage. They felt they had achieved spiritual maturity.

Paul warned the Corinthians about this attitude in verse 14. He did so in a tender and gentle way. He reminded them that they were "dear children" to him. He reminded them that he was their spiritual father in the faith. They had come to Christ through his ministry, and as a father, he expressed his deep concern for them.

As "teenagers" in the faith, the Corinthians felt that they had all the answers. They did not need Paul's parental guidance (see verse 8). Paul urged them to follow his example. He challenged them not to get caught into the trap of "comfortable faith." As believers, they needed to expect that, if they lived a godly life, they would be persecuted (see 2 Timothy 3:12). Paul did not hesitate to challenge the Corinthians to become imitators of him in his suffering (verse 16).

Paul believed that the Corinthians needed to break the shackles of *comfortable Christianity*. Despite his persecution, Paul was free. The Corinthians, on the other hand, though they considered themselves to be kings, were in reality chained and imprisoned in arrogant attitudes. In order that they be set free from these chains, Paul decided to send Timothy to them (verse 17). Timothy would teach them how they needed to live as true children of God. Notice that Paul did not single out the Corinthians for special teaching. What he told them was what he taught everywhere he went.

The challenge of Paul is for us as well. Paul desired to see people moving forward in the work of God. He challenges us here to move beyond our petty arguments and comfort zones. Some of the Corinthians had become arrogant (verse 18). They felt they had arrived. They had the right talk and knew the right doctrines. Paul was not interested in their talk. He wanted to see the power of God demonstrated in their lives. He wanted to see them put their talk into action. "The kingdom of God," said Paul, "is not a matter of talk, but of power" (verse 20).

This is a challenge to us today. How easy it is to stand on the sidelines and criticize those who are doing the work. This is what the Corinthians were doing. They stood at a distance and compared Paul to Apollos. They criticized those things that did not satisfy their preferences. They had all kinds of opinions concerning how things needed to be done. The fact of the matter, however, was that they did not lift a hand to do anything themselves. How often do we practice our Christianity by sitting in meetings and talking about how things should be done? Where are those who will move from talking about their faith to demonstrating their faith?

Paul believed that this was a very serious matter. He reminded the Corinthians, as their spiritual father, that if they did not change their ways, he would be forced to come to them with his whip (verse 21). May God challenge us to leave our comfortable pew in order to demonstrate in real life the power of the faith we profess.

For Consideration:

• What would Paul have to say to the church of our day? Have we become comfortable? Do we live as spiritual kings in our churches today?

• What are the real spiritual needs in your community? What is your church doing to demonstrate the power of God in addressing those needs?

• How has the power of God been demonstrated in your life?

For Prayer:

• Ask God to forgive us for becoming comfortable and thinking more of ourselves than we ought to think.

• Ask God to show you the real needs around you. Ask him to show you what he would have you to do about those needs.

• Ask him to demonstrate through you the real power of the gospel to change lives.

9

Old Yeast

Read 1 Corinthians 5

We have seen that the church of Corinth had problems with worldliness (3:1) and division (3:3) in their midst. Despite these sins, however, they had become quite comfortable with where they were in their spiritual development (4:8). Paul reminded them that their sins were even more extensive. In chapter 5, we discover that there were reports of gross immorality in their midst, as well.

The immorality found in their assembly was of such a nature that even pagans would be horrified (verse 1). It was reported that there was a man among them who was having sexual relations with his father's wife. It should be understood here that the phrase "father's wife" does not necessarily imply that the person concerned was his mother. In addition, we do not have any indication from the passage of where the father was at this time. Could he have died? Had he divorced his wife? Were they still living together? We are simply not told. We should not try to make this sin worse than it was. It is sufficient to note that such relations were strictly forbidden, not only by the culture of Corinth but also by the law of God in Leviticus 18:8.

What disturbed Paul about this situation was that the church of Corinth had not disciplined this brother. "And you are proud!" said Paul in verse 2. We saw in the last meditation that the believers in Corinth felt good about themselves. Paul had already told them that they were very proud (4:18). Here again he reminded them of their pride. In reality, however they had no reason to be proud. Instead of being ashamed of what was happening in their midst, they swept this matter under the carpet and ignored it.

Before we condemn the church in Corinth for their sin, it would be good for us to look at our own churches. Have we, like them, been guilty of ignoring sin in our midst? There are many reasons why we do not confront sin in the church today. Sometimes it is because of a lack of clear teaching of the Word of God. There are shepherds who simply do not have enough understanding of Scripture to know what God requires. Sometimes we choose to ignore the clear biblical teaching because we love our sin too much. Other times we do not deal with the sin because we do not have the courage to face those who are living in sin. The fear of people's reactions is more powerful than the fear of God.

Paul informed the Corinthians how they should have dealt with this situation. Let's examine what Paul taught them here.

Grieve in Your Hearts for the Sin (verse 2)

Paul began by telling the Corinthians that when they saw a flagrant and rebellious sin, their first response should have been to grieve. How often have we become calloused to the sin that surrounds us? Even in the church, we have accepted defeat as being normal. Somehow, we do not live with the understanding that victory is not only possible but also required. God does not delight in his people falling into sin. He has given us his Spirit to enable us to live in victory. His strength and power are at our disposition. It should grieve us to see Christians not availing themselves of this power to overcome sin.

Does your heart break when you see believers living in sin? Do you have a holy hatred for all that is contrary to the will and purpose of God? I am not sure what grieves me more in this passage—the sin of the man committing immorality or the sin of the church in not grieving. Before we can exercise any discipline in the church, we need to be a people who grieve over sin.

Judge the Sin (verse 3)

We will come back to verse 2 in a moment. In verse 3, Paul told the Corinthians that though he was not physically present with them, he had already passed judgment on this man. Satan would have us believe that we are not to judge anyone. He reminds us of our own unworthiness. He has believers so afraid of making any kind of judgment that they would prefer to leave sin alone rather than deal with it. All of this works to Satan's advantage.

Paul was not afraid to call sin *sin*. He could pass judgment on this man because this immorality is in direct contradiction to the clear teaching of the Word of God. When a brother or sister is violating the principles of the Word of God, it is our obligation to judge their sin accordingly and warn them. As believers, we need to judge everything according to the teaching of the Word. To refuse to do so is to play into the hands of the enemy.

Paul did not hesitate to judge sin. He encouraged the Corinthians to do likewise. When we refuse to judge sin, we choose to accept it and live with it. Soon the church is filled with sin and all standards are cast aside There will be times where we will be called to confront the enemy and make a judgment call about sin in our midst.

Put the Sinner Out of Your Fellowship (verse 2)

Having made a judgment, according to the Word of God, about sin in their midst, Paul then told the Corinthians to separate themselves from the sin and the sinner. He challenged them in this particular case to put the guilty man out of their fellowship.

Satan will not hesitate to remind us of the love of God when it suits his purpose. How often has he been successful in having us believe that putting a person out of the church would not be the loving thing to do? He would have us believe that it would be more loving to let the person stay in sin than to have victory over it. Deep in our hearts, we know that this is a lie, but we still struggle with it every time we need to exercise church discipline.

Separation must take place for three reasons. First, it reminds individuals of the seriousness of sin. This time of separation from the church should give them time to realize that they need to be serious about their Christian lives. They cannot live in sin and maintain fellowship with God and his people. If the individuals are serious about their faith, they will deal with their particular sin. Discipline shows them that sin is a serious matter that will not be tolerated in the church.

Second, discipline maintains the witness of the church. Probably one of the greatest accusations of unbelievers against the church of our day is the fact that there are too many hypocrites. This is due, in large measure, to the fact that as believers we do not exercise proper discipline in our midst. If we want to maintain our witness in the world, we need to deal with the sin in our assemblies.

The third reason we need to separate the sinners from the body is that it prevents further contamination of the church. Sin, like a contagious disease, has a tendency to spread. When we allow sin to run unchecked in our churches, it will soon take over. Like bad weeds in the garden, sin needs to be pulled up by the roots, or it will soon begin to choke the life out of the good plants.

In verses 6–8 Paul compared sin to yeast. When we put yeast in our bread, it quickly spreads through the whole loaf. This is what happens with sin. It is important that we deal with sin immediately. We cannot allow it to spread.

This principle of separating ourselves from the sinner is to be applied to those who practice rebellious and open sins in the church. Paul reminded the Corinthians that they could not apply this to the unbeliever in the world. If believers tried to separate themselves in this way from the world, they would have to leave the world itself (verse 10). As a people who lived in this world, they had to associate with the unbelievers.

There is a different standard for believers. The Corinthians were not to associate with those who claimed to be believers but did not live according to the moral standard of God's Word (verse 11). Paul listed particular sins here: sexual immorality, greed, idolatry, slander, drunkenness, and swindling.

Paul was not saying here that if a brother does not agree with us over a minor doctrinal or practical issue that we are to separate from him. Paul spoke here about clear violations of the moral standard of God's Word. Paul already condemned the church for being divided over these small and insignificant issues (see 3:1–4). Much damage to the witness of the church has come about because we have not been able to distinguish moral sin from differences of opinion over insignificant issues.

Hand the Sinner over to Satan (verse 4–5)

Paul told the Corinthians, finally, that they were to hand this man over to Satan for the destruction of the sinful nature. This merits some careful consideration. Notice in verse 4 that the handing over to Satan took place in the power and authority of the Lord Jesus. While the man was being handed over to Satan, he was yet in the hands of God. This passage reminds us of Job. Job was handed over to Satan. Satan was given the right to inflict and oppress Job for a time. God, however, did not take his hands off Job. Satan could only go as far as God allowed him to go.

It is clear in Scripture that even Satan serves the greater purposes of God. God allowed Satan to physically afflict Job so that God's greater purposes could be accomplished. God sent an evil spirit to oppress his servant Saul in order to show the world that his hand was on David (1 Samuel 18:10–16). God allowed Satan to inspire the evil kings of Babylon and Assyria to attack his own people in order to judge them and convict them of their sin (Jeremiah 25:9–12). God allowed Satan to sift Peter like wheat, even allowing him to deny Christ in order to break Peter of his pride (Luke 22:31–32; Matthew 16:23). God allowed a "messenger of Satan" to torment Paul so that he would trust only in the enabling power of God (2 Corinthians 12:7–9). Does it surprise you that God would use Satan to accomplish his greater purposes? Be encouraged that even Satan is subject to the greater purposes of God.

Notice the purpose of handing this man over to Satan: his sinful nature would be destroyed but his spirit would be saved on the day of the Lord (verse 5). Satan could not take his salvation away. God would use whatever Satan did to purge and cleanse this man of his sin.

So how does this discipline work in the life of the church if a man refuses to give up his sin? First, the church would attempt to deal with this man's sin according to the principles of Matthew 18:15–17. If he resists all the efforts of the church to bring him back to holiness, the man is removed from the fellowship and blessing of the church. He is committed into the hands of the Lord. The church is to pray that God would do whatever it takes to break the sinful nature that blocks this man from fellowship. Over the course of the next few weeks, months, or years, Satan and his angels are given limited access to this man, under the control of the Lord. The demons are delighted to inflict physical and even emotional pain on his body in their attempt to break him. Through this process and by means of the consistent prayers of the people of God, this man's rebellion is broken. He comes to see where his sin has led him. Broken in spirit, body, and soul, like the prodigal son, he realizes that what he had with his heavenly father was far greater than what he presently experiences. In humility and with a broken and contrite heart he returns to the fellowship of the body of Christ with a new awareness of his need. This whole process is exercised in love with the return of the sinner to fellowship as the central focus.

For Consideration:

- Why is it so difficult for us deal with sin in our midst? What keeps us from exercising discipline in the church today?

- What does this chapter teach about the importance of dealing with sin in our assemblies?

- Have you ever been handed over to Satan? What was the result in your spiritual life?

- What has been the result of rampant sin in the life of the church today?

For Prayer:

- Do you know believers who are living in sin today? Take a moment to pray that God would do whatever it takes to bring them back to himself.

- Ask God to forgive us as a church for not taking this matter of sin seriously.

- Ask God to raise up churches in our midst who take this matter of sin seriously.

10

Lawsuits among Believers

Read 1 Corinthians 6:1–11

The church in Corinth was far from perfect. We have seen that they struggled with division (3:1–4). In the last meditation, Paul encouraged them to deal with a man caught in immorality. Here in this section of 1 Corinthians, Paul unveiled yet another abominable practice. It appears that disagreements were so strong between certain believers that they were taking each other to civil court.

Paul had some strong words to say about this practice. "If any of you has a dispute with another, dare he take it before the ungodly for judgment instead of before the saints?" Paul asked (verse 1). In saying this, Paul recognized that there would be disputes between believers. Those disputes at times could be serious. He warned the Corinthians, however, about taking these cases to unbelievers to settle.

It should be mentioned that Paul was not telling the Corinthians that they should separate themselves completely from the secular judicial system of their day. In Romans 13:3–5 the apostle challenged believers to submit to the secular government that God had placed over them: "For rulers hold no terror for those who do right but for those who do wrong. . . . He is God's servant, an angel of wrath to bring punishment on the wrongdoer. Therefore, it is necessary to submit to the authorities, not only because of possible punishment but also because of conscience." Paul taught that the secular judicial system was from God and was to be respected. Even Christians are to respect the laws of the land or risk being condemned by the secular courts. The problem in the church in Corinth, however, was not that Christians were using the courts of the land to deal with legal matters. The problem was that they were not able to solve their problems among themselves. Paul condemned the practice of taking other believers to a secular court for two reasons.

Saints Will One Day Judge the World (verses 2–5)

The first reason why believers should not take each other to court, according to Paul, was that they would one day judge the world. Jesus told his twelve disciples in Matthew 19:28: "I tell you the truth, at the renewal of all things, when the Son of Man sits on his glorious throne, you who have followed me will also sit on twelve thrones, judging the twelve tribes of Israel."

Revelation, chapter 20, paints a picture of believers reigning with Christ in the millennium. The apostle John saw the thrones of those who were given authority to judge (Revelation 20:4). The Lord told the church of Laodicea that if they overcame, he would give them the right to sit with him on his throne (Revelation 3:21). Paul reminded the believers in 2 Timothy 2:12 that if they endured they would also reign with Christ. These verses and others remind us that the day is coming when those who truly belong to the Lord Jesus will one day rule with him. Paul told the Corinthians that believers will even judge angels (verse 3). The angels referred to here are very likely the fallen angels (Satan and his demons).

What a glorious thought this is. One day we will reign with Christ and participate with him in the judgment of the earth. If we are going to be part of the judgment of the entire world in the final days, can't we deal with these trivial cases among ourselves right now? This was Paul's appeal to the Corinthians. If they had disputes over trivial matters, they should have appointed even the least esteemed among them to deal with these issues, instead of going to civil authorities (verses 4–5). Wasn't there anyone among them who was wise enough to deal with these problems without having to go to the unbelieving courts?

As believers who were one day going to reign with Christ, the Corinthians should have been able to deal with problems among themselves. God had given them his authority to deal with any matter that stood between them. There was no need for them to go to the unbeliever for wisdom to settle disputes in the church.

Our Witness to the Unbelieving World (verses 6–8)

There is another reason why believers should not take each other to the secular courts. In verse 6, Paul reprimanded the Corinthians for going to secular courts in front of unbelievers. There is a tone of shame in Paul's words. How much damage has been inflicted on the cause of Christ by believers who could not accept their differences? What kind of witness is it to the world when believers make their conflicts public?

The fact that the Corinthians had lawsuits among themselves showed that they were already defeated (verse 7). They were defeated in their witness before the world. They were defeated in their relationships as believers. They were defeated in their walk with their Lord.

Paul reminded the Corinthians that it would be better for them to be wronged and cheated than for them to return evil for evil. How easy it is for us to claim our rights. Paul encouraged the Corinthian believers to turn the other cheek. He told them that it was better to suffer wrong than to retaliate and add their own sins to the sins of those who have wronged them.

Paul concluded this section by reminding the Corinthians that the wicked would not inherit the kingdom of God. He reminded them of their past before they came to know the Lord (verses 9–10). Before they came to the Lord, they were guilty of sexual immorality (adultery, prostitution, and homosexuality). Others were idolaters. Still others had been rescued from being thieves, alcoholics, slanderers, and swindlers. Since coming to the Lord, however, they had been washed and sanctified. God had worked in their lives and set them free from their former practices. They no longer had to live in these sins.

In the church of Corinth, however, the reality of the matter was that they had never learned to live in the victory that was theirs in Christ. Paul had already told them that they were still worldly (3:1). Paul did not question their salvation but certainly cast doubt on their maturity. In verse 11 he reminded them that they were washed (forgiven of their sins), sanctified (set apart for God), and justified (declared to be in a right relationship with God). As children of God, however, they had a long way to go.

How sad it is to see believers who are not experiencing victory over sin in their lives. We do not have to live with our sins. In Christ there is absolute victory. Here before us we see a picture of believers who were living in defeat. The Corinthian believers who were going to judge the world could not even judge the trivial matters that came between them. They were not living in victory in their relationships with each other.

For Consideration:

• Can you remember the last time you were wronged or falsely accused? What was your response to this?

• Can you remember a time when you were wronged and you took matters into your own hands? What was the outcome? Would it have been better for you simply to suffer wrong?

• Are there areas of your life where you are living in defeat? What are those areas?

For Prayer:

- Take a moment to ask the Lord to help you live in victory. Thank him that this is his heart for you.

- Do you know a believer who is not presently living for the Lord? Take a moment to ask the Lord to show them the victory that is theirs in Christ.

- Ask the Lord to heal relationships that are not what they should be in your life.

11

Sexual Immorality

Read 1 Corinthians 6:12–20

Paul has been challenging the Corinthians to deal with sin and hindrances in their spiritual lives. It appears from the opening chapters that there were many such issues in Corinth. We saw in the last meditation that many of the Corinthians had come to the Lord out of immorality and great sin (see 6:9–11). Could it be that these lifestyles had become the norm in Corinth? They needed some guidelines to follow as they sought to live for the Lord and walk in his ways.

Paul began his exhortation by giving the Corinthians two basic principles to follow in their relationship with the Lord and with others. "'Everything is permissible for me'—but not everything is beneficial. 'Everything is permissible for me'—but I will not be mastered by anything" (verse 12). Paul reminded the believers in Corinth that they were free in Christ. They were no longer under the law. In Christ they were free to enjoy the good things God had given them. They did not need to be overly concerned about what they could or could not eat or what they could or could not do on certain days of the year. While they were free, this did not mean that they could do whatever they wanted. Paul gave the Corinthians two guidelines to determine whether what they were doing was acceptable of not.

Is It Beneficial? (verse 12)

While I may have freedom to practice something, not everything I practice is beneficial for me or those around me. Reading is a wonderful pastime. We know, however, that not all reading is beneficial. Maybe you are involved in a legitimate activity that takes you away from your wife and family. In this case, your activity may not be beneficial to them. We should ask ourselves the question: Is what I want to do going to be beneficial to me and to those around me? Paul reminded the Corinthian church that there would be times when they needed to stop doing something because it was not personally beneficial or it did not benefit those around them. They were to consider the effect of what they did on others. It was better not to practice something that would cause a brother or sister to stumble. Paul encouraged the Corinthians to turn away from those things that were not beneficial.

Will I Be Mastered by What I Do? (verse 12)

Paul challenged the Corinthians to ask themselves secondly if they would be mastered by the activity they practiced. If we are honest with ourselves, sometimes we enjoy certain things too much. Even legitimate activities can become gods to us. The moment we begin to see things controlling our time, resources, and energy, we need to take a break from them. This can be true of religious activities as well as secular. For a long time in my life, I was mastered by "business" for the Lord. I wanted to do everything I could for him. Paul said to beware of anything other than God himself that dominates and masters your time, energy, and resources.

From this opening statement, Paul went on to speak more directly of sexual immorality (verse 13). "'Food for the stomach and the stomach for food'—but God will destroy them both. The body is not meant for sexual immorality, but for the Lord, and the Lord for the body." What was Paul telling the Corinthians? Notice how Paul said that food was for the stomach and the stomach for food. This is quite easy to understand. The stomach has a particular function in the body. Its purpose is to digest food. The stomach was made for food. In a similar way, the body has a purpose. Our bodies are given to us so that with them we can serve the Lord. Just as the stomach was made for food, so our bodies were made for the Lord and his glory. To use the body for sexual immorality would be to dishonor the body God gave us and to use it in a way it was never intended to be used. Paul then moved beyond this argument to show the Corinthians that sexual immorality was wrong for four other reasons.

We Will Be Raised (verse 14)

This physical body with its needs will one day be decayed by death. When the Lord Jesus came to this earth and died for our sins, he died so that we could have victory over sin and death. The power that raised the physical body of the Lord Jesus from the grave will one day raise our physical bodies as well. As believers, we have a wonderful hope. We will be raised to spend an eternity with Christ. What motivation this ought to give us to live in light of that hope. Those who live in light of eternity will keep their bodies pure for the Lord.

Our Bodies Are Members of Christ (verses 15–18)

The second reason why the Corinthians needed to flee from sexual immorality was that they were members of the body of Christ. The day they accepted the Lord Jesus as their Savior a radical transformation took place. The apostle Peter put it this way in 1 Peter 2:9: "But you are a chosen people, a royal priesthood, a holy nation, a people belonging to God, that you may declare the praises of him who called you out of darkness into his wonderful light."

As a chosen people, the Corinthians had been called from darkness into a deep and personal relationship with God. As unworthy as they were, they stood before a dying world as God's representatives and children. They would reign with him throughout eternity. God was pleased to call them his own.

Would it be right, asked Paul, to take a member of the body of Christ and join that member to a prostitute? Would this not be blasphemous? All sexual immorality is sin, but for believers this sin is particularly heinous because it profanes the Lord Jesus with whom they are joined in a pure union. Sexual sin is the most destructive, both physically and spiritually.

Our Bodies Are the Temple of the Holy Spirit (verse 19)

The third reason why the Corinthians were to flee sexual immorality was that their bodies were the temple of the Holy Spirit. When they became children of God, the Lord sealed the transaction by placing his Holy Spirit in their hearts to empower and enable them to live as he required. As believers, their bodies were the dwelling place of the Holy Spirit of God. Should we defile the temple in which God's Spirit dwells? On the contrary, we must honor God by the way we care for and use our bodies.

You Were Bought with a Price (verse 20)

Before coming to Christ, the Corinthians lived in immorality and sin. The Lord Jesus rescued them from the bondage of that sin. He set them free at the cost of his life on the cross. He died that they could be forgiven and live in a new way. Knowing the cost of their redemption, how could the Corinthians return to the life they once knew? They had an obligation to walk in purity of life.

What a privilege it is to be part of the family of God. Our bodies are the dwelling place of God's Holy Spirit. We stand before the world as his representatives. As caretakers of the dwelling place of God's Spirit, we are called to live in such a way that the Lord Jesus is glorified in our bodies. For this reason, Paul said we must flee sexual immorality.

For Consideration:

- ✱Take a moment to consider how you make decisions. Apply the principles in verse 12 to how you live your life. *What would it look like if we applied the principles in v. 12*
- ✱How does knowing that you belong to Christ and that the Holy Spirit lives in you affect what you do with your life? Is there anything in particular that the Lord would have you change?

For Prayer:

Our bodies as a temple ~ Food (read devotional)

- Ask God to reveal to you any areas in your life that need to ✱ be changed in light of the teaching of Paul in this chapter.

- Thank the Lord for the transaction that took place on the cross.

- Thank him that his Holy Spirit dwells in you to empower and enable you to live for him.

- Ask God to enable you to live a pure and holy life.

" We cannot give our hearts to God but keep our bodies for ourselves"
What does it look like for you to honor God with your body.
— love who he has created me to be
— make wise food/exercise choices.

12

To Marry or Not To Marry

Read 1 Corinthians 7:1–9

In chapter 7, the apostle Paul spent time trying to answer some questions that had been sent to him in a letter from Corinth (verse 1). In verses 1–9, the apostle answered a question concerning whether it was better for a person to marry or not.

In answering this question, Paul began by stating his personal preference: "It is good for a man not to marry" (verse 1). What Paul said here seems to contradict the teaching of Genesis 2:18 in which God stated: "It is not good for the man to be alone." What was Paul telling the Corinthians here?

The answer to this seems to lie in verse 7. While the sex drive is normal and natural and finds its ultimate satisfaction within the context of marriage, some individuals have received from God the gift of celibacy. Paul was one of those individuals.

According to Paul, marriage brings its obligations and concerns (see verses 32–35). A married person is concerned not only for the needs of the Lord but also for a partner and a family. The married person will not have the same time to spend on the things of God as an unmarried person. Paul told the Corinthians that it was good to be able to give themselves fully to the work of the Lord. As an unmarried person, Paul was unhindered by the constraints and obligations of family life. He was free to move as the Lord led him, with no concern about a wife and children. This was a good thing. Paul enjoyed the freedom to move as the Spirit of God led him.

Having said this, however, the apostle realized that not everyone had the gift of celibacy. There were those whose sexual needs were such that they needed to be married. Immorality abounded in the city of Corinth. While Paul believed that celibacy was preferable to marriage, he encouraged those who did not have the gift of celibacy to marry in order to avoid falling into sexual immorality. Only in the context of marriage could their sexual appetites be fulfilled in a God-honoring way. For this reason, he encouraged each man to have his own wife and each woman to have her own husband (verse 2).

Paul encouraged the husband and wife to fulfill their marital duties to each other (verse 3). The context indicates that this "duty" referred to sexual relations. Paul told the Corinthians that the wife's body did not belong to her alone but also to her husband, and the husband's body belonged to his wife (verse 4). There is an important principle that we need to understand.

Some see in this verse a license for one partner to demand his or her due from the other. This is not what Paul was teaching here. While writing to the Ephesians about marriage, Paul used a similar picture. Listen to what Paul said in Ephesians 5:28–29: "In the same way, husbands ought to love their wives as their own bodies. He who loves his wife loves himself. After all, no one ever hated his own body, but he feeds and cares for it, just as Christ does the church."

These verses help us understand what Paul was teaching in verse 4. Paul was saying that in marriage each spouse gives up exclusive rights over his or her own body. Marriage includes the loving care of each other's body. Spouses ought to be as concerned about the needs of their spouse as for their own needs. Paul's challenge to the married couple was to stop thinking selfishly. He challenges them to open their eyes to the needs of their partners and reach out to fulfill those needs as if they were fulfilling their own personal desires. Notice also that Paul gave equal rights to the wife and the husband. He did not regard one partner as having needs that the other did not have.

How many problems in marriage could be avoided if couples learned this principle of caring for each other in this way? Many a husband has watched his exhausted wife stand at the kitchen sink, washing dishes as he relaxed in his favorite chair. If he cared for his wife's body as his own, what would his response be? Would he not help her as he would want to be helped?

In light of this teaching, Paul exhorted husbands and wives to stop depriving each other of sexual relations. Instead, they were to care for each other's needs. There were exceptions to this rule. Paul realized that there were special occasions when a couple decided, by mutual consent, to cease having sexual relations. One example of this would be to spend time in prayer and seek God. Both partners, however, needed to agree to this. It was also understood that this agreement would only be for a certain time. They were to quickly return to their normal relations so that Satan would not tempt them and cause them to fall into immorality (verse 5).

What we need to understand from this is that Satan is looking for every opportunity to cause us to fall. It is his particular delight to destroy Christian marriages. If the couples concerned are spiritual leaders in the church, the break-up of their marriages will have devastating consequences in the whole church. We cannot allow Satan access to our marriages.

While Paul felt in his heart that it was better for believers to give themselves completely to the work of the Lord, he realized that not everyone had the gift of celibacy. For those who did not have this gift, it was better that they be married rather than to burn with passion and blaspheme the name of Christ by falling into sin (verse 9).

The believers in Corinth were living in a society filled with immorality. They needed to be godly lights in the midst of tremendous darkness. We have seen that immorality had been creeping into the church of Corinth. We too are seeing an alarming increase of sexual immorality among believers in our day. Even spiritual leaders are falling into this trap of Satan. More than ever before, we need to see healthy marriages in the body of Christ. We cannot invest too much into making our marriages better.

Paul taught that marriage, though not necessary for those like him, was necessary for others. He challenged married couples to be supportive of each other's needs. Paul knew that even those who were married could fall into sexual immorality and blaspheme the name of God.

For Consideration:

- Do you have the gift of celibacy? How do you know? What freedom has this given you in service for the Lord?

- Are you tempted by immorality? Where are your particular weaknesses?

- If you are married, take a moment to discuss what you have learned in this section with your partner.

- Do you care for your partner's needs as you care for your own? In which areas could you improve?

For Prayer:

- Ask God to help you to care for your partner's needs as you care for your own. Ask God to forgive you where you have failed in this.

- Take a moment to lift up the marriages of your spiritual leaders. Ask God to help your spiritual leaders to build strong marriages that would be examples to others.

- Ask God to forgive you for the times you have not loved your partner as yourself. Ask God to help you to make things right.

13

Sanctified

Read 1 Corinthians 7:10–24

After having dealt with the question of whether it was good for a man or woman to marry, Paul turned his attention to the married couples in the Corinthian church. In particular, he had some words for believers married to unbelieving partners.

There were obviously a number of believers in the church of Corinth who did not have a believing partner. What should they do? Should they continue to live with them despite their rejection of the Lord? Paul gave the Corinthians some basic principles to follow.

The Believer Must Not Separate from the Unbeliever (verse 10)

In verse 10, Paul told the believers that, as a general rule, they were not to separate from their unbelieving partners. The marriage vows made prior to conversion to Christ were still applicable. Believers were to continue to love and remain true to their unbelieving partners (verse 10). This would not always be easy. As believers, they had a new allegiance to God and his holy ways. Their partners, however, would not always understand or appreciate the changes in their lives. Sometimes unbelieving partners would become hostile to their newfound relationship with the Lord. Despite this difficulty, believers were to remain faithful in their marriages so that the name of the Lord would be honored.

Notice in verse 10 that this teaching was not originally from Paul but from the Lord Jesus himself (see Matthew 5: 31–32; 19:5–8). It is the will of God that believers remain true to their unbelieving partners. He who has called believers will also be faithful to them. He will give his children the strength necessary to be faithful in difficulties.

The Lord knows the pain we feel. He will not call us to do something he does not give us the strength to accomplish. We can trust him in all our trials.

If the Believer Separates, He or She Should Remain
Unmarried (verses 11–12)

Having stated the general principle, Paul understood that there would be situations where it was not possible to remain with an unbelieving spouse. We live in a sin-cursed world. It is possible, for example, that living with an unbelieving partner could compromise the safety or physical welfare of the family. There might be times when the unbelieving spouse would strike out against the believer with physical violence. Maybe the lifestyle of the unbelieving spouse would have a negative effect on the children and draw them away from the Lord. What does the believer do in such a situation? While Paul did not encourage the believer to separate from the unbelieving spouse, he realized that there were cases where this was inevitable. When separation was necessary, Paul permitted the believer to separate, remain unmarried, and seek reconciliation with the unbelieving spouse.

If the Unbeliever Wishes to Remain, the Believer Should Not
Seek Divorce (verses 13–14)

Paul made it clear that if the unbeliever was happy to

remain with the believing partner, then the believer was not to seek a divorce. Paul went on to explain that the unbelieving partner was "sanctified" through the believing partner and their children were "holy" before the Lord. In order to understand what Paul was saying, we need to see it in the context of the question being asked by the Corinthians. Were they living in sin because they were married to unbelievers? Were the children of this partnership legitimate?

Paul told the Corinthians that their unbelieving partners were sanctified or set apart by God. In other words, God recognized, under the circumstances, that these unbelievers were legitimate marriage partners, set apart for special blessings by being married to Christians. The children of this union, as well, were holy or legitimate children. Since God accepted the union of their parents, the children were also accepted as the legitimate fruit of their relationship. The entire family would receive many blessings because of the presence of even one believing parent. Paul encouraged believers, therefore, to remain with their unbelieving partners because God accepted their union and would set it apart for special grace.

If the Unbeliever Leaves, Let Him or Her Go (verses 15–16)

While faithfulness to marriage vows was to be encouraged, if the unbeliever chose to leave the marriage, the believer was to allow him or her to do so. In such a case, the believer was no longer bound. "God has called us to live in peace," Paul said in verse 15. The believer was not to try to hold on to the marriage against the will of the unbelieving spouse. "How do you know, wife, whether you will save your husband? Or, how do you know, husband, whether you will save your wife?" Paul asked in verse 16. While every effort should be made to bring the spouse to Jesus, there was no guarantee from God that this would ever happen. If an unbeliever was unwilling to live with a believing partner, it was better to divorce and be at peace. A believer, however, did not have the option of initiating divorce (see verses 10–11).

Remain as You Were Before You Came to Know the Lord (verses 17–24)

Paul concluded his challenge to married couples by stating that believers should remain in the status they were before they came to know the Lord. If they were uncircumcised when they came to know the Lord, said Paul, they should not be circumcised simply to be like their friends. If they were slaves before they came to know the Lord, they should not demand to be free. They should serve the Lord as slaves with all their hearts. Slaves could take comfort in knowing that in Christ they were free. Believers were to remember that their calling to serve the Lord did not depend on their social status. The Lord called them to service in whatever condition they were currently living.

How many times have we lost opportunities to be lights in this world because we have assumed that becoming a Christian meant leaving everything we came from? We *are* to leave our sin and our sinful lifestyles. But God wants us to remain, as much as possible, in the circumstances we were before coming to the Lord, so we can minister to the people in that setting.

Paul's challenge to the believer married to the unbeliever was to be faithful to the marriage vows and consider it a privilege to minister to the unbelieving partner for the Lord. God considered their union binding. At the same time, however, Paul called for peace in the relationship. There were times when separation was unavoidable. God would not hold the believer bound to a relationship from which the unbeliever chose to permanently separate.

For Consideration:

• Do you have an unbelieving spouse? What are some of the special challenges of living with an unbeliever?

• In what ways do you believe that your relationship with the Lord has brought blessing to your unbelieving spouse and your children?

- How much contact do you have with the people of your unbelieving past? Is there any way that you can be a light to them today?

For Prayer:

- Do you have an unbelieving spouse? Take a moment to pray that God would give you the grace to remain faithful to your wedding vows.

- Ask God to help you to be a positive witness to your unbelieving spouse.

- Pray for someone in your unbelieving past. Ask God to show you if there is any way that you can be a light to them.

14

Happy Celibacy?

Read 1 Corinthians 7:25–40

Paul had been answering some questions the Corinthians had asked concerning marriage. Here in this next section of chapter 7, the apostle sought again to address the question of whether it was good to marry. His answer came in three parts.

Consider the Present Crisis (verses 25–31)

If the Corinthians were undecided about whether they should marry, they should consider their answer in light of the present crisis (verse 26). Notice in verse 25 that while Paul did not have a particular command from the Lord about this matter, his advice to remain single was sound counsel and was included here by God in Scripture. Because this was not a command, those who chose to marry would not be sinning (verse 28).

What was the crisis Paul spoke about in this passage? The context gives us the answer. In verse 29 Paul reminded his readers that the time was short. In verse 31 he told them that this present world is passing away. Paul had a very deep sense of urgency in his task of reaching the world for Christ. Paul lived his life with the awareness that the Lord could return at any moment, and this demanded sacrificial living.

There was much to be done in light of the coming judgment. Unbelievers needed to be warned. Even believers needed to be prepared to meet their God. This was not a time to be wrapped up in the luxuries of life. This was a time for intensifying efforts in preparation for the Lord's return. It was with this in mind that the apostle challenged the unmarried ("virgins," verse 25) to remain unmarried.

In verse 29 Paul said: "From now on those who have wives should live as if they had none." Paul was not counseling believers to abandon their spouses here. He was simply reminding them that while, in normal times, they might have time and resources to please each other, now the time was short. As couples, they needed to sacrifice some of those luxuries for the sake of reaching this world. People should not use marriage as an excuse for not being devoted to the Lord's work.

Because Paul knew he was living in a world that is passing away, he urged believers not to get caught in the emotions of this life. Paul said that those who mourned should get over their sadness and press on in the work of reaching the world (verse 30). Those who were happy and joyous needed to realize that this was not the time for celebration and partying. Those who delighted in buying the good things of this world needed to be willing to sacrifice their resources to reach this world in need of a Savior. This was not the time to be engrossed in the cares and possessions of this world.

We must admire the dedication of the apostle Paul to the cause of reaching the world for Christ. The understanding that this world is passing away radically affected his lifestyle. How does your passion for the world compare to the apostle's passion? It is true that nearly two thousand years have passed since Paul wrote this, and the Lord has not yet returned. Yet, the coming of Jesus is even closer, and so our urgency in reaching the world for Christ should be even greater.

How much have you become engrossed in the cares of this world, including questions of marriage? Paul challenged the Corinthians to answer that question in light of the present spiritual crisis in the world. We might mention again that Paul was not saying that those who marry are sinning or less spiritual than those who choose a life of celibacy. He made this clear in verse 28. He simply challenged them to consider the possibility that maybe they could better serve the Lord in these last days by remaining single.

Consider the Additional Responsibility (verses 32–35)

Paul challenged the Corinthians to consider the additional responsibility and burden placed on a married person: "An unmarried man is concerned about the Lord's affairs—how he can please the Lord. But a married man is concerned about the affairs of this world—how he can please his wife— and his interests are divided."

Any married couple comes to understand that marriage does not just happen—it requires a lot of work and sacrifice. Molding two personalities into one is not ever easy. Then there is the responsibility of bringing up children to know and love the Lord. There are many worries and concerns for the married couple. A married person is legitimately concerned about the welfare of his or her spouse and children. A married person's interests are divided. An unmarried person can devote mind, soul, and body to the work of the Lord. Before deciding to marry, Paul challenged the unmarried to consider the added responsibility they would have in the care of their spouses and families. If they married, Paul told them, they would have to divide their attention between the work of the Lord and their families.

It is not always easy to maintain balance in ministry, even as a single person. The needs of people shout from all directions. The demand for our time is sometimes more than we can handle. The burden for people can absorb all our energy. Added to this, however, married people must address the needs of their spouses and children. These needs in themselves can take almost all their time and energy. Paul wanted to spare the Corinthians the added burden of family.

Consider Your Own Conscience (verses 36–40)

Finally, Paul told the Corinthians that before deciding to marry, they should consider their consciences. In verse 36 he said, "If anyone thinks he is acting improperly toward the virgin he is engaged to, and if she is getting along in years and he feels he ought to marry, he should do as he wants. He is not sinning. They should get married."

Paul was telling the Corinthians here that each person needed to consider his or her conscience before God in this matter of whether or not to marry. Paul told the Corinthians that it was not a sin to marry, and it was not a sin not to marry. Ultimately, this question needed to be decided on an individual basis with the Lord. If individuals felt that they were acting improperly by not marrying, then they ought to proceed with marriage. If, on the other hand, they had control over their bodies and minds, then they should consider giving themselves completely to the work of the Lord without the restrictions of marriage (verse 37).

Paul teaches us here that not everyone is called to marriage. Before assuming that you have to be married, ask God if marriage is his purpose for your life. You should only be married if this is God's purpose for your life. If it is, then you need to commit yourself to that marriage for life. Remember, Paul told the Corinthians that a man or woman is bound to a partner as long as that partner is alive (verse 39). When you marry, you make a life-long commitment. Only the death of a spouse should break that commitment. At the death of a partner, the remaining partner, according to Paul, is free to remarry. Paul believed, however, that the believer would be happier to remain single.

In conclusion, the apostle said that this question of whether a person should marry needed to be taken seriously. Before making a life-long commitment to a partner, Paul challenged his readers to consider whether this was actually the will of God for their lives. He challenged them to consider whether it would be more appropriate for them to devote themselves to the work of the Lord without the restrictions of family life.

For Consideration:

- Consider for a moment the devotion of the apostle Paul to the cause of reaching the world for Christ. What challenge does this bring you personally?

- Are there things that you would struggle to give up for the cause of Christ?

- Have you been called to marriage? How do you know?

- If you are married, what particular challenges do you face in balancing your commitments?

- How are you ministering to the needs of your spouse? How can you minister more effectively to each other as a couple?

For Prayer:

- If you are married, ask the Lord to help you find the balance between serving the Lord and ministering to your partner and children.

- If you are not married, ask the Lord to show you if it is his purpose that you marry.

- Ask the Lord to give you a deeper sense of urgency in the work of reaching this world for Christ in these last days.

15

Sacrificial Meat

Read 1 Corinthians 8

In chapter 7, the apostle Paul answered a series of questions related to marriage. Here in chapter 8 he addressed the issue of meat sacrificed to idols. In the pagan culture of Corinth, believers frequently came into contact with this type of meat. When sacrifices were made to idols, a portion of the sacrifice went to the priests, and some of it was sold in the marketplace. The Corinthians wanted to know if it was acceptable for them to purchase this meat. Did believers defile themselves by eating meat that had been offered to idols at pagan temples?

Before answering these questions, Paul made an important point in verse 1: "Knowledge puffs up, but love builds up." Let's break this statement down to understand what Paul was saying.

Knowledge Puffs Up

Knowledge is a wonderful thing when it is used properly. There is something about knowledge, however, that can lead to pride. Even a little knowledge can cause us to think more highly of ourselves than we ought to think. Our knowledge can cause us to lose patience with those who do not understand the things we understand. It can separate believers and cause them to look down on one another regarding various issues of faith.

Before giving instruction on this matter of food sacrificed to idols, the apostle Paul wanted to remind the Corinthians of the danger of knowledge. Paul realized that the truth he was going to share could be divisive. Paul could imagine people latching on to what he said and looking down on those who were not yet ready to receive that truth. To counter this Paul had two things to say.

First, if we think we know something, we probably still have a long way to go (verse 2). The greatest lesson that Bible college and seminary taught me was how much I did not know about the Bible. As years have passed and I have grown in my understanding of the Word of God, I now have more questions than I ever had. The more we know, the more we come to realize what we do not know.

As I mature, I am coming to realize that not everything in life is clearly defined. I find myself saying, "I don't know," more frequently. Paul wanted his audience to beware of the arrogant person who had an answer for everything. There is always more to learn on every subject.

Second, Paul reminded the Corinthians that God knows those who truly love him (verse 3). What is important in life is that we love God and are known by God. The Christian life is not about knowledge—it is about love for God. The apostle John reminded his readers that if they loved God, they would also love others (see 1 John 2:9–11). Paul seems to have been warning the Corinthians about the knowledge he was going to teach them. He wanted to make sure that the Corinthian believers would not take this knowledge and use it in an unloving way.

Having warned them about the dangers of knowledge without love, Paul proceeded to explain his understanding of food sacrificed to idols. The truth of the matter was that idols are nothing (verse 4). An idol is simply a piece of wood or stone. In itself, it has no power. It was true that these idols had the names of certain gods associated with them, but the Corinthian believers knew that these were false gods (verse 4). There was only one true God (verse 6). This one true God was the source of all life. Why should a believer be concerned about food offered to a certain false god that had no power?

It is important that we examine what Paul was saying here. Should we draw the conclusion from this that believers do not have to get rid of objects in their homes associated with pagan worship? Is it okay for us to bring things into our homes that can become tools of Satan?

When we served as missionaries on the island of Reunion in the Indian Ocean, we rented a house that belonged to a very superstitious property owner. She had placed religious medallions over all the doors and windows of the house to ward off evil spirits. Other religious objects were hung in various places in the house for protection and blessing. I have never lived in a house that had such an obvious sense of spiritual oppression. We felt as though we were living under a dark cloud. While these objects did not have any power in themselves, I believe that they provided an entrance for demonic spirits into the house. The only way for us to break the oppression we felt in that house, was to remove these objects. When we did, the oppression ceased.

Throughout the Old Testament, the Lord challenged his people to rid their homes and their nation of all objects associated with the pagan religions around them. There is a difference, however, between participating in pagan and ungodly practices and buying meat in the marketplace. The people who bought meat in the marketplace had only one motive. They wanted to feed their families. For Paul, they did nothing wrong by eating meat with this motive.

There are times, however, when the believer must take a stand and refuse the ungodly practices of paganism. In the illustration I used earlier about the superstitious property owner, my wife and I believed that by removing these charms, we were stripping Satan of his hold on that house. We must cleanse our lives and homes of anything directly related to evil and sin. Those who ate meat sacrificed to idols, however, were not doing anything ungodly. They were not opening their lives to Satan. They were just buying groceries at the market. This meat would not hinder their spiritual journeys or promote evil.

Love Builds Up

Having shared his knowledge on this issue, Paul proceeded to remind his readers that true love builds up (verse 1). There were individuals who struggled with eating anything that was sacrificed to idols. Their consciences would not permit them to eat such food (see verse 7). While Paul believed that this food would not harm them, he exhorted his readers to show compassion and love towards those who did not have this opinion. While the Corinthians had freedom to eat this meat, they were to be careful not to place a stumbling block in front of a weaker brother or sister.

The knowledge that Paul shared with the Corinthians had the potential to *destroy* the faith of weaker believers (verse 11). It could possibly lead such an individual to return to idol worship. If this happened, the offending party would have to answer to Christ for his or her actions. Knowledge without love and compassion is very dangerous. It would be far better never to eat meat sacrificed to idols than to eat it and cause a brother or sister to stumble and fall. Compassion must rule knowledge. Paul warned the Corinthians that by hurting a brother or sister, they were sinning against Christ (verse 12).

Paul assured the Corinthians that eating meat sacrificed to idols would not hurt them spiritually if they had clear consciences. At the same time, however, there were believers who did not have this type of faith. In these cases, love for these believers was to take priority over the liberty and freedom in Christ to eat this kind of meat. Paul called for a community in which love for others took precedence over personal freedoms.

For Consideration:

- What has been the result of knowledge without love and compassion in the church today?

- To what contemporary issues in the church today does this teaching apply?

- What is the difference here between eating meat sacrificed to idols and allowing sinful and evil practices into our homes and lives?

For Prayer:

- Ask the Lord to help you to find a balance between knowledge and compassion for the people around you.

- Ask God to give you a greater understanding and love for weaker brothers and sisters.

- Ask him to forgive you for the times you have been arrogant and not shown compassion and understanding to others.

16

A Personal Example

Read 1 Corinthians 9

P aul had taught the Corinthians that while they had freedom to eat meat sacrificed to idols, it was not always the proper thing to do. Their compassion for others would sometimes lead them to forfeit their rights for the sake of a weaker believer. Here in chapter 9, the apostle shared a personal example from his own life of this principle. He reminded the Corinthians of how, as an apostle, he had sacrificed certain rights and privileges for them.

Paul began by reminding the Corinthians of his position in the body of Christ. He was an apostle (verse 1). As an apostle, he was an authoritative witness to the person of the Lord Jesus. He had seen the resurrected Lord Jesus on the road to Damascus. Paul's call as an apostle gave him a particular status in the body of Christ. The Corinthians had seen the evidence of the Lord's hand on the life of Paul. He had ministered among them for a year and a half (see Acts 18). Many of the believers reading this letter had come to the Lord because of Paul's ministry in Corinth. The Corinthians were the fruit of Paul's ministry and a confirmation to him of his particular calling to be an apostle (verse 2).

Not everyone accepted the apostle Paul. We are told in verse 3 that there were some who judged him. We are not told what these individuals had against the apostle. Paul's focus here, however, was not to defend his ministry but to share a personal example of how believers need to be willing to sacrifice personal freedom for the good of the body.

Paul reminded the Corinthians that, as an apostle, he had the right to take a wife with him on his journeys. Many of the other apostles brought their wives along with them on their journeys (see verses 5–6). Paul, on the other hand, chose not to marry. We saw in chapter 7 that it was his desire to give himself entirely to the work of the Lord. The Corinthians had benefited directly from Paul's decision not to marry, as did many other churches. No other apostle seemed to have had the impact this man had. His decision to not marry set him free to bring great blessing to many churches.

As an apostle, Paul also had the right to "food and drink" (verse 4). In other words, he had the right to receive wages for his labor of love. Even their own culture taught them that a laborer deserved his wages. In verse 7, Paul gave a series of examples of this from Corinthian culture. Does a soldier serve "at his own expense?" Doesn't his country pay his wages and provide him with the weapons necessary for its defense? Have you ever met a person who planted a vineyard who was forbidden the right to eat the grapes that grew in that vineyard? How about the shepherd who tended a flock? Does that shepherd not have the right to drink milk from that flock?

From these examples, the apostle moved to the teaching of the Old Testament law itself (verses 8–12). He reminded his listeners of what Moses said regarding the muzzling of an ox while it was treading the grain. The law stated that the ox was to be allowed to eat the grain he trod (Deuteronomy 25:4). The farmer was not to muzzle the working animal, preventing it from eating. Paul told the Corinthians that this passage was not simply about cruelty to animals. It was given to teach that those who worked ought also to share in the harvest of their labors.

The practical application of this was that because the apostle had sown spiritual seed in their midst, according to the law of God, he also had the right to share in a material harvest. In other words, he had the right to be paid for his services in Corinth. Even the priest of the day had a right to a portion of the sacrifices offered on the altar (verse 13). Paul reminded the Corinthians that the Lord Jesus taught that those who preached the gospel had the right to earn their living from the gospel (see Luke 10:5–7).

While he had this right, Paul chose not to use it (verse 12). Instead, he put up with the resulting hardships so that he would not hinder the preaching of the gospel to those who heard him. He was not in ministry for the money. He served the church out of a passion for his Lord and for those lost in sin. He would minister whether he received a salary or not.

Paul willingly sacrificed his privilege to receive a salary. He preached because he was called of God to preach, not because he was being paid to do so (verses 16–18). If Paul had preached for selfish purposes, he would have demanded payment. But Paul preached out of the will of God in a stewardship of trust. Being able to offer the gospel free of charge was all the reward Paul desired.

There is a valuable lesson here in this passage for us. Would you, as a servant of God, minister to a people if you knew they could not pay you for your services? Is your sense of calling greater than your wallet? The apostle Paul had been set free from the love of money and possessions. He sacrificed his right to a wage and offered himself freely to the body of Christ. His sacrifice brought great blessing to the church. How we need to have more individuals like this in the body of Christ.

Paul's ministry was one of sacrifice. This was one of the reasons for his success as a missionary. To the Jew, he became like a Jew. To those under the law of Moses, he lived like one under the law. To the weak, he became weak. He was willing to become all things for all people (although Paul would have never violated God's moral law) so that he might win them to the Lord (verses 19–23).

How easy it is to have our own ideas of how things ought to be. I have met individuals who, having chosen to live in a particular income bracket, refused to sacrifice their lifestyle. There are others who refuse to leave the comfort of their own culture to serve on the mission field. Still others have become so stuck on their traditions and ways that if the Lord called them to something else, they would refuse.

In his ministry on this earth, the Lord Jesus was often accused of breaking the traditions of the fathers. He seemed to stretch people beyond their comfort zones. He still does this. Where are those who will willingly sacrifice their reputations, their bank accounts, their comfort zones, and their time for the Lord Jesus? Could it be that the reason we are not seeing the success that Paul saw is because we are unwilling to make the sacrifices he made?

The apostle concluded this section with an example from the world of sports (verses 24–27). There are many people who run a race, Paul said. Only one of those people will get the prize. Those who are serious about the race will discipline their bodies and make many sacrifices in order to win the victor's crown. This is what Paul did. He disciplined his body and made it his slave so that he might win many to the Lord. He did not run the Christian race aimlessly. He had a goal of expanding God's kingdom and disciplined himself to attain that goal. Is that your heart?

Paul refused to be entangled in the cares of this world. His sacrifices made a profound impact on the world for Christ. If eating meat is going to cause your brother to stumble, then don't eat meat. If standing up for your rights will hinder the communication of the message, then sacrifice your rights. This was Paul's lifestyle. This was his challenge to the Corinthians.

For Consideration:

- Is there anything in your life that you would personally have difficulty sacrificing for the Lord? What is it?

- Has there ever been a time when you were not able to follow the leading of the Lord because you felt it would cost you too much? Give an example.

- Is there anything in particular that the Lord would have you to sacrifice for him so that his work will move ahead in a greater way?

For Prayer:

- Ask the Lord to free you from the love of possessions and worldly comfort.

- Ask God to reveal to you anything that would stand in the way of greater service for him.

- Take a moment right now to offer your life and your possessions to God. Tell him that you will allow him to take away anything that would hinder you in your service of his kingdom. Ask him to give you a heart like the heart of Paul.

17

A Warning from History

Read 1 Corinthians 10:1–13

It is easy to read the pages of Scripture and see the sins of others but fail to see our own sins. We can often think more highly of ourselves than we ought to think. We can think we are strong in our faith, but then we fall into sin. Here in this section of Scripture, the apostle Paul gave the Corinthian believers a lesson in history as a warning to not fall back into the idolatry of the surrounding culture.

Paul began by reminding the Corinthians of how their spiritual ancestors were "baptized" in the cloud and in the sea (verses 1–2). This seems to refer to the time when the Israelites crossed the Red Sea after leaving the land of Egypt. Paul was drawing a parallel between the experience of the Corinthians and the experience of the Israelites in the wilderness.

The Corinthians had lived in sin and the bondage of idolatry just as the Israelites had lived in the bondage and slavery of Egypt. One day the Lord sent Moses as a type of savior to rescue the Israelites from their bondage and take them to the Promised Land. The Israelites identified with Moses as their leader, and Paul referred to Israel's passing through the Red Sea as a type of baptism into Moses.

In a similar way, the Corinthians had been baptized into Christ as a symbol of their freedom from the bondage of sin. Now like their spiritual ancestors, they too had chosen to follow their Savior to the Promised Land.

As the children of Israel wandered through the wilderness on their way to the Promised Land, they ate the same spiritual food and drank the same spiritual drink (verses 3–4). This seems to refer to the manna the Lord supernaturally provided each day. On at least two occasions, God provided water from a rock to quench their thirst. Through their wilderness wanderings, the children of Israel experienced the wonderful provision of the Lord. As followers of the Lord God, the Israelites experienced the power and presence of the Lord in a way they had never before experienced him. The food and drink had spiritual significance in that they pointed to Christ—the actual sustainer of God's people (verse 4; see John 6:32–35).

The Corinthians were having a similar experience. We will see later in this book that, as a church, they experienced very powerful demonstrations of the Spirit's gifting. They also shared communion at the Lord's Supper, eating spiritual food and drinking spiritual drink. Similar to their spiritual ancestor of old, the Corinthians were experiencing exciting times.

Paul went on to say that God had not been pleased with the people of Israel. Despite their newfound freedom and the evidence of God's presence and power in their midst, all but two of them suffered the judgment of death in the wilderness. Paul was warning the Corinthians that the same thing could happen to them if they were not self-disciplined in their freedom. These things happened to ancient Israel as an example for the Corinthians and all the Lord's people (verse 6).

What was it that caused Israel to fall and perish in the wilderness despite their deliverance and evidence of God's power in their midst? Paul listed four sins that caused the Lord to judge the Israelites.

They Set Their Hearts on Evil Things (verse 6)

Throughout their history, the children of Israel set their eyes on the nations around them. On one occasion, they asked the Lord for a king because they wanted to be like the rest of the nations (1 Samuel 8:4, 5). The sinful ways and practices of the nations held a certain attraction for the Israelites. They had lived in Egypt for hundreds of years amid great idolatry and immorality. Although the Lord had delivered them out of this pagan culture, the Israelites still lusted after the evil ways of Egypt.

The Corinthians were struggling with similar things. They had been delivered out of the pagan culture of Corinth, but they were still lusting after their old ways of idolatry. By eating meat offered to idols and attending pagan feasts at the temple (8:10), some were in danger of falling back into idolatry. In chapter 3, Paul spoke of the Corinthians as being worldly. The quarrels they experienced among themselves were because they had been setting their minds on evil things. They had become proud and arrogant. They had not really allowed the Lord to transform their minds and hearts.

They Practiced Idolatry (verse 7)

The children of Israel turned their backs on the Lord God to serve other gods. Soon after leaving the land of Egypt, they set up a golden calf idol to worship. Later on, they would bow the knee to Baal. They would even offer their children as sacrifices to Baal.

Idols abounded in Corinth too. Paul had spoken in chapter 8 about eating food sacrificed and served at the pagan temples. The temptation was never far away to return to the worship of these idols. "Do not be idolaters," Paul told them. Notice that part of the idolatry involved eating, drinking, and "indulging in pagan revelry." Satan made idolatry look very exciting. Paul challenged the Corinthians not to fall into his trap. The same temptations existed in Corinth that caused ancient Israel to fall.

They Were Guilty of Sexual Immorality (verse 8)

The people of Israel coming out of Egypt were also guilty of sexual immorality. One of the characteristics of the worship of Baal was its immoral sexual practices. Temple prostitutes were a vital part of the worship of Baal. The priests of Baal themselves engaged in ritualized sexual practices to guarantee the harvest for the coming year. The children of Israel found this hard to resist. Numbers 25:1–9 speaks of a time when the men of Israel engaged in sexual immorality with Moabite women who invited them to the sacrifices to their gods. All these men were put to death.

Paul spent much time in this letter exhorting the believers in Corinth to live according to the standards of the Word of God regarding their sexual conduct. They were not to conform to the standards of their pagan society. There was already evidence of sexual immorality in the church of Corinth (chapter 5). This was an area of deep struggle for the Corinthian church, as it had been for Israel. The sins that had caused Israel's downfall could also cause the fall of the church in Corinth.

They Tested the Lord and Grumbled (verses 9–10)

Paul reminded the Corinthians of how the children of Israel tested the Lord by grumbling and complaining against him. He reminded them of the story in Numbers 21 where the children of Israel complained to Moses about their wilderness hardships. They told Moses that they had been far better off in Egypt. This so angered the Lord that he sent venomous snakes to bite them. They tested the Lord by the way they refused to trust him. They tested the Lord by the way they complained about what he was doing in their midst.

In Corinth the believers were also guilty of testing the Lord. They did this by the divisions in their assembly. Brothers and sisters were taking each other to court. They tested the Lord by their complaining about their spiritual leaders. "I am of Paul, I am of Apollos," they said. There were those in the church that did not like the way Paul did things. All this grumbling and complaining about what was happening in their church tried the patience of Almighty God.

All these things were written in Scripture to teach lessons of faithfulness to the children of God (verse 11). They still serve as warnings to us in our day. The church of Corinth had fallen into the trap of the same sins as ancient Israel. The Corinthians were guilty of lusting after evil things, idolatry, sexual immorality, and testing the Lord by their complaining and grumbling.

How easy it is for us to read the pages of Scripture and not see history being repeated in our own lives. We read about the sins of the children of Israel or the church of Corinth, and we are horrified at what we read. What we fail to see, however, is that our society and church are equally as guilty. If you think you stand, be careful lest you fall, Paul told the Corinthians in verse 12. Why would Corinth stand when Israel fell for the same sins?

Paul concluded this section with an encouraging word for those who were struggling with these particular temptations. There is no temptation, he said, that God will not give you the strength to overcome. God will never let you be tempted beyond your ability to resist. He will always provide a way of escape for you (verse 13).

The problem is that, while God provides the way of escape, we are often unwilling to take that escape. If we are honest with ourselves, the reason we fall into sin is ultimately that we want to sin. If we were truly seeking victory, we would take advantage of the means of escape that God provides.

Ultimately, like ancient Israel and Corinth, we are without excuse. God has left us with examples in Scripture that serve as stern and clear warnings. He has promised a means of escape from each of the temptations that come our way. It is up to us to learn from these examples and turn from sin.

For Consideration:

- The apostle James compared the Word of God to a mirror. Why is it so hard for us to see ourselves in the pages of this inspired Word?

- What idols do we face in the church today?

- Have you ever found yourself grumbling and complaining about your spiritual leaders, the church, or your "lot in life?" What is the challenge of this passage to you?

For Prayer:

- Ask God to forgive you for the grumbling and complaining you have done against his servants, his church, and his will for your life.

- If you are presently struggling with a temptation, ask the Lord to show you the means of escape.

- Thank God that he promises a way of escape from temptation.

18

The Bounds of Freedom

Read 1 Corinthians 10:14–33

P aul had challenged the Corinthians regarding their rights and freedoms as believers. In chapter 8 he showed them that they had the freedom to eat meat sacrificed to idols. In chapter 9 he spoke to them about his personal freedom as an apostle. It would be easy for some to find here an excuse to practice whatever they wanted without restraint. In order to counter this, Paul had reminded the believers in the opening section of chapter 10 of their spiritual ancestors who abused their freedom without restraint. The result was that they had all perished in the wilderness. True freedom must have its boundaries. Paul provided two boundaries to spiritual freedom in this section.

You Cannot Drink the Cup of Demons and the Cup of the Lord (verses 14–22)

First, while Paul had no problem with the Corinthians eating food sacrificed to idols, he made it very clear that they were to flee idolatry. In order to illustrate his point, the apostle Paul used the illustration of the Lord's Table.

What did the Table of the Lord represent for the Corinthians? Paul reminded them that as they drank the cup and ate the bread, they were symbolically participating in the blood and body of Christ. In other words, they were, by this practice, recognizing that it was for them that the Lord Jesus had died. In participating in the Lord's Supper, they were accepting the work of the Lord as their only hope of forgiveness and cleansing from sin. Paul also reminded them that because the bread they ate was part of one single loaf, they had unity in the Lord (verse 17).

To illustrate this further, Paul challenged the Corinthians to "consider the people of Israel." When they ate the sacrifices that were offered on the altar, were they not identifying with what had happened on that altar? In the sacrificial system of the Old Testament, when an animal was sacrificed, part of the animal went to the priest, and, in certain sacrifices, the people offering the sacrifice ate part of the sacrifice. As they ate this offering, they rejoiced together over the goodness of God and the forgiveness of their sins. They identified themselves with the death of the animal and ate the remainder as an act of thanksgiving and worship to the gracious Lord God.

The sacrifices that the pagans were offering in Corinth were to demons (verse 20). The actual idol was merely wood or stone with no power in it. But behind that idol was a deceiving demon of hell that was holding the worshipers captive. By offering sacrifices to these idols, the worshipers were surrendering and submitting themselves to the demons of hell.

If, as Paul said, behind these idols were the demons of hell itself, would it not make sense that believers reject the practice of idolatry. Paul told the believers to not drink the cup of demons and also the cup of the Lord (verse 21).Would this not arouse the jealousy of a holy God (verse 22)? If his jealousy was aroused, would anyone be strong enough to stand against him? Even common sense told the Corinthians that it would be both evil and dangerous to offend a holy God by the practice of idolatry.

In the exercise of our freedom, we must be sure that we do not arouse the anger of the Lord. We need to remember what the Lord has done for us in redeeming us from sin. We need to live our lives doing only those things that bring honor and glory to him and his Word. Flee from the practice of idolatry. Bow the knee to the Lord God alone.

Everything Is Permissible but Not Everything Is Beneficial (verses 23–33)

Second, Paul told the Corinthians that everything was permissible. Paul was making a general statement here. He obviously did not mean that they could do anything they pleased. He had just told the Corinthians that they were to flee idolatry. So we can assume that idolatry is not permissible for the believer. The Corinthians were free to enjoy the good things the Lord had given unless, of course, those things were contrary to his Word. For Paul, the Christian life was not a set of laws and regulations but freedom through Christ and for the glory of Christ.

While the Corinthians had been set free under Christ, not everything was beneficial. Not everything would build up the body of Christ. In the exercise of freedom, the Corinthians were to seek the good of others. Paul went on to explain what he meant by giving the Corinthians an example from everyday life.

When the Corinthians went to the market to buy meat, they could keep their consciences clear by not asking whether it was sacrificed to idols (verse 25). Because the earth and everything in it belongs to the Lord, they were free to enjoy the good things the Lord had provided for them. Even if they were invited to a meal at the home of an unbeliever, they should not worry about where the meat came from (verse 27). They were free simply to enjoy the hospitality of their host. If, however, another person told them that the meat they were buying or eating had been sacrificed to idols, for the sake of that person, they should not eat the meat (verse 28).

We may have the freedom to do something in the privacy of our own homes that we would not do in the company of others. It is better to sacrifice our personal freedom than to offend a brother or sister who does not have this freedom. By practicing our freedom in public, we risk creating a problem for a weaker believer who will judge us for doing what they consider evil (verse 29). If we thank God for a meal that offends weaker people, they will denounce us (verse 30). This will only bring unnecessary separation between true believers.

Paul summed up his teaching on freedom in verses 31–32. He told the Corinthians first that whatever they did they were to do for the glory of God (verse 31). Second, he told them that in everything they did, they should be careful not to place a stumbling block in front of another person, whether that person was a believer or an unbeliever. Paul made it his goal in life to do nothing that would cause another person to fall. He did this so that others might be saved (verse 33).

Paul encouraged the Corinthians to live in the freedom of Christ and to enjoy the life the Lord had given them. While they were free in Christ, they were never to worship that freedom. Like Paul, they were to be ready in an instant to sacrifice their rights and freedoms if, by so doing, they would bring greater glory to the Lord.

For Consideration:

- What are the idols we have to deal with in our day? Is there an idol that you need to deal with in your life?

- Would you be willing to sacrifice your personal freedoms for a brother or sister in Christ?

- Is what you have freedom to practice beneficial to those around you? If not, what should you do?

For Prayer:

- Ask the Lord to help you hold your personal freedom lightly.

- Have you ever been a stumbling block for another person? Ask the Lord to forgive you.

- Have you ever become negative or critical of another believer who had the freedom to practice something you did not have the freedom to practice? Ask God to forgive you and give you a better attitude toward that person.

19

Women's Head Coverings

Read 1 Corinthians 11:1–16

P aul moved on in chapter 11 to address the question of women and men in the church. Paul began by commending the Corinthians for observing his teaching elsewhere (verse 2). The assumption was that they would also listen to his teaching regarding the roles of men and women in the church. Paul made it clear that what he shared with them was not his own understanding but the instructions of the Lord.

He began with a parallel: "The head of every man is Christ, and the head of the woman is man, and the head of Christ is God" (verse 3). Paul was teaching the Corinthians that there is a God-given order in the church. Headship does not imply superiority. Just as Christ is not inferior to his Father because he submits to his will, so a woman is not inferior to man in her submissive role. Just as Christ and the Father are equal, so men and women are equal. God has ordained, however, that men and women exercise different roles in the body of Christ. Men have been given the role of "head." Their role model is the person of the Lord Jesus. Christ's headship was exercised through humble service to the church. As head, Jesus willingly died for the church. The leadership role is a role of service.

Paul continued in his discussion by introducing the topic of women wearing head coverings in public worship. Obviously, women were questioning whether they should wear head coverings, as was the custom of the day. Some may have dispensed with the head covering and come to worship with their heads uncovered. This was causing a problem in the church of Corinth. In the last few chapters, Paul had reminded the Corinthians that they needed to be willing to sacrifice their rights and freedoms if those freedoms caused a stumbling block for another believer. Were there women in the church of Corinth who were unwilling to sacrifice their freedoms for the good of others?

In verse 4, Paul told the Corinthians that a man who prayed or prophesied with his head covered dishonored his head. It is clear from the context that the covering of the head was a sign of respect and submission in their local culture. To uncover the head was to take authority. A woman coming into the church with her head uncovered was making a public statement in that day. She was symbolically asserting her authority and rebelling against her God-ordained submissive role in the church. For a man to cover his head was a symbol of his refusal to take authority. In so doing, he was disregarding his God-given leadership role. It would be a shame for a man who had received authority from the Lord to refuse to take that authority.

History indicates that in the Corinthian culture, a woman's hair was a source of great pride. To shave a woman's head was to disgrace her. In verse 6, Paul told the women of Corinth that if they did not wear a veil, they should have their heads shaved. In other words, they should be ashamed of themselves for their rebellion. Just as it would be a shame for a woman to have her head shaved, so it would be a shame for her to take off her veil in public worship. Paul exhorted the women of Corinth to wear their head coverings as a sign of submission to the God-ordained leadership roles in the church.

According to Paul in verse 7, a man did not need to wear a head covering because he was the image and glory of God. Though men and women are equal before God, it was man who was created first and given authority over the earth. Woman, on the other hand, was the glory of man. What was Paul saying here? He was *not* saying that God considers women to be second rate. He was simply reminding the Corinthians of the roles God had given to men and women. God created man first from the dust of the earth. Woman was created from man and was created to help him. Man was not created for woman but woman for man (verse 9). This fact alone, for Paul, was significant and had implications in the church of Jesus Christ regarding the roles of males and females.

God created man for the purpose of bringing glory to his name. God created woman to be a partner with man in that task. Man is the glory of God in the sense that he had been chosen by God to represent him in this world. Woman is the glory of man in that she was chosen by God to assist man in that same undertaking.

Both men and woman ought to be happy with the roles God has given them from creation. When a woman in Corinth wore a veil, she was saying that she was happy to accept her role. The head covering represented her submission to God-ordained male leadership in the expansion of the kingdom.

In verse 10 the Corinthian women were exhorted to wear a "sign of authority" because of the angels. Angels watch over the affairs of God's servants in the church. Angels might be present in its worship and service assemblies. If angels were present, it would be inappropriate for a woman to resist God's purpose by refusing to wear the sign of her submission. To do this would offend the angels who had come to help and protect believers in the worship and service of God.

Having explained to the Corinthians the importance of respecting their God-given roles within the body of Christ,

Paul wanted next to make it clear that both men and women needed each other. Paul stated that originally woman came from man (verse 12). On the other hand, however, a male child is conceived in the womb of a woman and without her, he would not have life. Men and women are mutually dependent one on the other from the beginning of life. This is how it ought to be in the church. God has created us in such a way that we owe our lives to each other. Having different roles does not mean that one sex is more important than the other, and it does not mean that one role is more spiritually important than the other.

Paul concluded this section by encouraging the Corinthians to judge this matter for themselves (verse 13). He told them that nature teaches that there is a distinction between the sexes. One of these distinctions is the hair. While men have a tendency to go bald, women almost never lose their hair. Women generally take more pride in their hair than men. Paul said that God has given a woman a natural covering for her head that is her pride and glory. That natural head covering, according to Paul, is a symbol of her role as an essential partner to man in glorifying God in the world and in the church (verse 15; see Genesis 1:28).

Paul knew that his teaching on this subject would not be well accepted by everyone. To those who resisted his teaching, Paul simply said that this was the teaching and practice of the church (verse 16). In other words, this matter was not open for discussion. This was where the apostles stood.

What do we take from this section of 1 Corinthians? We learn that there are different roles in the body of Christ for men and women. God has determined that men should exercise the role of headship in the church. Women should help men in this task. Each sex is to honor God by fulfilling an individual role.

The issue of head covering has been a controversial matter in the church for centuries. Is it necessary for women to wear head coverings in worship today? Those who believe women should wear head coverings take these verses at face value. They see them as applying directly to the church of our day as well. They encourage each woman to wear a head covering as a symbol of an acceptance of God's order in the church.

Those who do not feel that a head covering is necessary generally base their arguments on two facts. First, Paul told the Corinthians that a woman's long hair was a natural head covering (verse 15). Second, the head covering was a culturally understood practice in the time of Paul. In different parts of the world, a head covering may not have the same cultural significance. It is also quite possible for a woman to wear a head covering and not be submissive in her heart. Would this hypocrisy not bring even greater dishonor to the name of the Lord?

In the culture of Corinth, a woman refusing to wear a head covering would have caused quite a stir. In fact, it would have been distracting to the worship of God. It was an outright statement of rebellion against male headship and the clear teaching of the Word of God. For this reason, Paul exhorted the women of Corinth to wear head coverings.

For Consideration:

- Do you believe that women should wear head coverings today? Why or why not?

- Are there any cultural equivalents to a head covering in your culture?

- What practices in the church today can hinder the presentation of the gospel to our culture?

- How should this principle of male headship be worked out in the context of the church? What is the role of women?

- How has the principle of male headship been abused in the church?

For Prayer:

- Ask the Lord to help you take your role in the body of Christ seriously.

- If you struggle with Paul's teaching here, ask God to give you grace to obey even though you do not fully understand.

- Thank the Lord for the role of his angels as we worship and serve him.

20

The Lord's Supper

Read 1 Corinthians 11:17–34

We have seen that there were many problems in the church of Corinth. In chapter 1 Paul addressed the issue of division among believers. In chapter 3 he told them that the source of the jealousy and quarrelling among them was their worldliness. In chapter 5 he addressed the question of immorality. They were reprimanded in chapter 6 for the lawsuits that were springing up between believers. In chapter 10 the apostle challenged them on the issue of idolatry. We saw in chapter 11 that women in Corinth were struggling with the teaching of Scripture regarding their role in the church. Here in this next section, Paul addressed yet another important issue in the Corinthian church, the misuse of the Table of the Lord.

Paul began by telling the Corinthians that in this matter, he had no praise for them (verse 17). The apostle told them that what they were doing was causing great harm to the body of Christ. The problem Paul referred to had as its root the disunity that existed among the believers. They were divided over their leaders. They were divided because of the lawsuits among them. They were divided over the practice of eating meat sacrificed to idols. They were divided over the issue of the role of their women in the church. We will see later on in this book that they were also divided over the use of spiritual gifts. Many issues divided the church of Corinth.

These differences were being seen in the practice of the Lord's Supper. Notice in verse 21 that some people were eating without waiting for others. Paul went on to say that one person was getting drunk while another remained hungry. We need to understand that the practice of the Lord's Supper was different from our modern practice. This remembrance of the Lord would have been part of a larger meal. It was in the context of such a meal (shared by the disciples in the upper room, Mark 14:12–26) that the very first celebration of the Lord's Table occurred. For the early church, it would have been quite normal to have the celebration of the Lord's Table in the context of a church supper. As the assembly gathered for this common meal and the remembrance of the Lord's death, some believers were getting there before others and began eating and drinking without concern for those who would come later.

Verse 22 indicates that what they were doing was humiliating those who had nothing. This has led commentators to believe that what was happening was that the rich were coming early to these meals and not waiting for the poor people who had to work long hours. The result was that the rich were feasting and getting drunk so that there was nothing left to eat or drink when the hard-working poor people arrived later. We can only imagine the division this caused in the church of Corinth. This was obviously not the context for remembering the Lord's death. Some were drunk with too much wine while others were bitter because they had nothing to eat or drink.

Paul rebuked the Corinthians for what was happening. He challenged them to remember that they were to come together as one body of Christ in which no social distinctions exist. They were to equally share in the Lord's Supper. Their unloving behavior was blasphemous. By their practice they showed that they despised the church and the poor. This was contrary to everything the Lord Jesus represented. Paul told those who were practicing gluttony to eat and drink at home before they came.

Having reminded the believers of the problem, Paul then moved on to show them what the Lord's Supper represented. Paul told the Corinthians that he had received from the Lord the things he was passing on to them. What he told them about the Lord's Supper was not his own idea; it was from the Lord himself (verse 23).

It is important that we realize here that Paul was not with the disciples on the day the Lord instituted the Lord's Supper in the upper room. It would be easy for some that had their doubts about Paul to criticize what he said here because he was not one of those twelve disciples. Paul removed any doubt from their minds with this statement.

Paul reminded the Corinthians that on the night Jesus was betrayed, he took bread and broke it, telling his disciples that this bread represented his body. He then commanded his disciples to eat this meal in remembrance of him. After the supper was over, Jesus took a cup and told those present that the cup represented a new covenant in his blood. The old covenant requiring sacrificed animals was about to be fulfilled. A new covenant between God and his people was about to be established by the blood of Jesus Christ. It was the clear teaching of the Lord that whoever ate this bread and drank this cup was proclaiming the death of the Lord Jesus until he returned. The memorial of the Lord's Supper was a celebration of the meaning and the benefits of the death of the Lord. It was a serious commemoration of gratitude and proclamation of the gospel. But the Corinthians had turned it into an occasion for gluttony and drunkenness, which was more in line with the pagan celebrations.

The apostle concluded by giving the Corinthians a stern warning about their practice of the Lord's Supper. He reminded them in verse 27 that whoever drank the cup of the Lord in an unworthy manner would be guilty of sinning against the body and blood of the Lord. This was a serious matter. By their selfish behavior at the Lord's Supper, they were degrading the very body and blood that saved them. Paul challenged them to examine themselves before they participated in the Table of the Lord (verse 28). Those who ate and drank indifferently, without honoring the holy body and blood of Christ, were eating and drinking judgment on themselves (verse 29). Paul went on to say that this was the reason why some among them were sick. Some had even died as a judgment of God for their blasphemous actions at his Table (verse 30). Paul associated their physical illnesses with their profane actions at the Lord's Supper.

What a powerful lesson this would have been to the Corinthians. I can imagine some of those who had been involved in these blasphemous practices being struck with the connection between their sickness and their improper practice of the Lord's Supper. While we should not always assume that all sickness is the result of sin in our lives, the Bible does teach us that there are times when the Lord does discipline us in this way.

Paul challenged the believers in Corinth to realize the seriousness of what they were doing. This section was a wake-up call to those who were guilty before the Lord. The hand of the Lord was on them in judgment. Some of them were sick, and some of them had died because God had not taken their blasphemy lightly. Having failed to judge themselves, they were judged by God. The Corinthians were guilty of sinning against the body and blood of Christ and sinning against their fellow believers. Paul taught here that the observance of the Lord's Supper is a powerful reminder of the gospel and an effective motivator for living a disciplined and loving life.

For Consideration:

• What does the Lord's Supper mean to you?

- What does this section teach about sickness as a discipline of God? Can you ever recall a time when God used sickness to draw you back to himself?

- What are some ways we can be guilty, like the Corinthians, of participating in the Lord's Table in an unworthy manner?

For Prayer:

- Have you ever been guilty of participating in the Lord's Table in an unworthy manner? Take a moment to confess your sin to God.

- Take a moment to thank God for the death of his Son on your behalf.

- Ask the Lord to deal with any divisions between believers that exist in your church.

21

Spiritual Gifts

Read 1 Corinthians 12:1–11

Paul next dealt in some detail with the use of spiritual gifts in the body of Christ. Obviously, this had caused some concern for the believers in Corinth, and Paul did not want them to be ignorant about this matter. The question of spiritual gifts was so important that Paul devoted the next three chapters to this subject. He expected the Corinthians to pay special attention to his instructions.

Paul began his teaching on spiritual gifts by recognizing the background from which many of the Corinthians had come. They were a people who had been led astray by "mute idols" (verse 2). These idols had no power and could not speak, but still the Corinthians had once been led astray by them. How could these Corinthians discern what was from God and what was not? Paul reminded them in verse 3 that anyone who spoke by the Spirit of God would proclaim and recognize the lordship of Jesus Christ. The Holy Spirit would never lead anyone to curse either the work or the character of the Lord Jesus (verse 3). Those who depreciated or denied the person and work of the

Lord were not speaking from God.

In order that the name of Christ be exalted, God distributed to the church those gifts he deemed necessary (verse 11). Notice what Paul said in verses 4 and 5. There are different gifts from the same Spirit. The Greek word for gifts in verse 4 is the word *charismata,* meaning "divine grace," from which we get the English word *charismatic.* These are divine abilities that enable believers to glorify Christ and serve in the church. There are also different kinds of services or ministry opportunities from the same Lord (verse 5). There are, thirdly, different kinds of "working" from the same God (verse 6). The "working" here may refer to the mighty power of God and is distinguished from the service opportunities of verse 5 and the more general charismatic gifts of verse 4.

Notice also in verses 4–6 that these gifts come from all the members of the Trinity. The Spirit gives gifts (verse 4); the Lord gives gifts (verse 5); and God the Father gives gifts (verse 6). This indicates that all three members of the Trinity are in harmony when it comes to the distribution of these gifts to the believer, the opportunities for ministry, and the empowerment for service.

Notice also that God works out these gifts in "all men" (verse 6). This indicates that God has given to each of us a gift that he wants us to use for the furtherance of his kingdom. Paul reminded the Corinthians in verse 7 that every believer is given a manifestation of the Spirit for the common good of the body. God has not left his servants without power but has equipped each one with the necessary tools to build up the body of Christ. Each believer makes a unique and necessary contribution to the common good, not just certain believers with the more spectacular gifts.

In verses 8–11 Paul gave some examples of the gifts that God has distributed to the body. This list does not contain all the gifts. We will look briefly at the gifts mentioned here.

Message or Word of Wisdom (verse 8)
Wisdom is the application of truth and knowledge to real-

life situations. The person with this gift is empowered by God to share words that direct the body of Christ in the application of the revealed truth. This person is not necessarily a teacher or preacher but has a very keen sense of how to apply knowledge to everyday situations.

Message or Word of Knowledge (verse 8)
The gift of the word of knowledge is the ability to unveil truth for the body of Christ. This knowledge may be very specific in nature. Jesus, for example, *knew* that the Samaritan woman had five husbands (John 4:18). He also *knew* that personal sin had not caused a certain man's blindness (John 9: 1–3). This knowledge may also be a supernatural understanding of the truth of God as contained in the Scriptures. The person with this gift is empowered of God to communicate the meaning of his Word.

Faith (verse 9)
While each believer has a measure of trust in God, there are those who have been particularly gifted to trust God in extraordinary ways. These individuals are able to attempt the impossible for God and see his blessing. Their answers to prayer and strength under pressure inspire others to have confidence in God and his provision.

Gifts of Healing (verse 9)
While in some ways this gift is connected to the gift of faith, its focus is on the sick. God gives to some people a particular burden to pray in his will for individuals that God himself desires to heal. Healing may involve physical, emotional, or spiritual issues. The fact that Paul used the plural when he spoke about this gift (i.e., *gifts* of healing) has led some to say that there are various types of healing gifts. Does God call some to a ministry of inner, emotional healing and others to a ministry of physical healing, for example? Others believe that the plural was used here because this gift is given many times to these individuals, as they need it. In other words, each time

God wants to use these individuals to heal, he gives them a gift to do so.

Miraculous Powers (verse 10)

Miracles are distinguished from healing here in that they are not related to the healing of the body, mind, or soul. Miracles relate to the changing of the normal course of nature. Jesus, for example, stilled the storm. He also raised the dead. Individuals with this gift are empowered by God to alter the normal course of nature for the purpose of expanding the kingdom of God and glorifying the name of Christ.

Prophecy (verse 10)

Prophecy, in the Scripture, was the ability to speak the word of God concerning a particular situation. While it may have had some future application, the majority of prophecy in Scripture related to the present. Prophecy, according to Paul, ought to strengthen, encourage, and comfort the body of Christ (14: 3). Prophets in the Bible were given the ability to hear God's word and communicate that word either to specific individuals or to the larger body of Christ. People with this gift are God's mouthpieces to communicate the truth of God to his people at a given time and situation.

Distinguishing between Spirits (verse 10)

In a very general sense, this gift is a God-given ability to discern whether a specific person or movement is of the Lord or of the enemy. It may also include the idea of being able to recognize and identify the presence of Satan in an individual or situation. Peter, for example, discerned that Ananias was being motivated by Satan to give a gift to the church (see Acts 5). Jesus discerned the hypocrisy of the Pharisees as they spoke to him on various occasions. Individuals with this gift have the ability from God to discern and identify the presence of evil or good in an individual or situation. They serve as guards for the body of Christ to warn of danger.

Speaking in Different Tongues (verse 10)

There appear to be two types of tongues in the Bible. The tongues of Acts 2 were known languages. The tongues of 1 Corinthians 14, on the other hand, were unknown languages. In Acts 2 the Holy Spirit gave the disciples the ability to speak words that were unknown to them but clearly understood by those present from many different language groups. The purpose of this gift in Acts 2 was the proclamation of the gospel in other languages. In 1 Corinthians 14, Paul spoke of a prayer language unknown not only to the speaker but also to those around him. The purpose of this type of tongue was not evangelism but worship, prayer, exhortation to the body (when interpreted), and personal edification. It may be that the reason Paul used the expression "different kinds of tongues" was to include the various types of tongues we have mentioned here. The person with this gift is given the ability to speak words unknown to him or her with the goal of furthering the kingdom of God in evangelism, exhortation, or personal edification.

Interpretation of Tongues (verse 10)

The interpretation of tongues is simply the ability to accurately translate the language spoken by someone speaking in tongues. This translation would serve for the edification of the larger body. This could take place in the context of a regular worship service, as recorded in 1 Corinthians 14, or possibly in a private situation. The person speaking in tongues may also be given the gift to interpret his or her own words (1 Corinthians 14:13). The person with this particular gift has an ability to understand the things that are spoken in these unknown tongues.

God gives to the body those gifts he deems necessary for the expansion of his kingdom. Ultimately, God himself determines what gift we will receive. We must be content to exercise that gift for the good of the body of Christ.

For Consideration:

• Why do you suppose there is a fear of the gifts of the Spirit in some circles in the body of Christ?

Spiritual Gifts ● 109

- Has God given you one or more of these gifts? What are they? How are you using these gifts for the good of the larger body of Christ?

For Prayer:

- If you do not know what gifts the Lord has given to you, take a moment to ask the Lord to show you.

- Thank the Lord that he is willing to use you in such a special way to extend his kingdom.

- Ask God to give you eyes to see the opportunities to use the gifts he has given you.

22

One Body

Read 1 Corinthians 12:12–31

Having shown that the Lord has distributed a variety of gifts to the church, Paul next taught the Corinthians how those gifts, though different, worked together for the common good of the body. To do this he used the example of the human body with its various parts and functions.

The human body is made up of many different parts, each with its unique function. This is what the body of Christ is like (verse 12). The body of Christ is composed of people from many different cultural and social backgrounds (Jews and Greeks, slaves and free). Each of these individuals has been baptized by one Spirit and drinks from that Spirit (verse 13). Let us consider this more carefully.

When Paul said that believers were all baptized by one Spirit into one body, he referred to the baptism of the Spirit, not water baptism. The baptism of the Spirit, according to this verse, occurs when the Holy Spirit comes to individuals, planting his life in them and making them children of God. At that time, the new believer is enabled and empowered to drink deeply from the well of salvation and experience all its benefits. What does this mean in practical terms?

At the point of conversion, the Holy Spirit comes to an individual, planting the life of Christ in that person's heart. In the days of Mary and Joseph, the Holy Spirit came to Mary and planted the seed of Christ in her womb. In a similar way, the Holy Spirit comes to plant the life of Christ in us today. The indwelling Holy Spirit lives in us to transform our characters by empowering us to obey God's ways.

This Holy Spirit baptized the Corinthian believers and brought them all into a common spiritual family. Paul taught that if people did not have the Spirit of Christ in them, they did not belong to Christ (Romans 8:9). The life of Christ in an individual is what makes that person a child of God.

What we need to understand here is that when the Holy Spirit comes to baptize each of us, filling us with Christ and his power, he does so in a way that is unique for each person. While filled with the same Spirit, each believer is unique. Though we are one body, there are many parts to that one body (verse 14). Each of those parts is essential for the proper functioning of the body. No part is inferior to another. For example, the foot cannot say, "Because I am not a hand, I do not belong to the body" (verse 15). Nor can the ear say, "Because I am not an eye, I do not belong to the body" (verse 16). This would be foolish indeed. Yet how often do we compare our gifts and ministries to others in the church and feel as though we do not belong?

Paul challenged this way of thinking in verse 17. What if the whole body were an eye, he asked. If the whole body were an eye, how could it hear? What if the whole body were an ear? How could it smell? The fact of the matter is that God has determined that the body be comprised of many different members. Each member is necessary for the full functioning of the body. The eye cannot say to the hand, "I don't need you." The head cannot say to the feet, "I don't need you."

If we were to compare the head and the feet, would the head not receive more honor than the feet? Yet the feet are no less important to the full functioning of the body. While the head does the thinking, the hands and the feet do the work. In the same way, there should be no envying in the body of Christ. Every person in the body has an important role to play. One gift is no better than another. All are important and essential to the full functioning of the church.

Have you ever stubbed your toe? While the toe is a seemingly unimportant member of the body, my whole body ceases to function for a moment when I stub my toe. The same is true when I hit my finger with a hammer. My heart begins to beat faster. The pain shoots down my arm, and then my feet begin to do a little dance. My head feels the pain and then my mouth and tongue cry out in agony. My whole body responds. For a moment (until I recover from the pain), the work I am doing is put on hold. This, said Paul, is how it is when even the seemingly unimportant gifts are not functioning in the body of Christ.

Do you feel that your gifts are not important? Paul's words should teach you that without your gifts (however small you feel they are), the body will not function as it should. Your gifts are essential to the proper working of the church. When your gifts are being used, you help bring health and wellness to the body of Christ. The whole body rejoices with you in health.

Paul told the Corinthians in verse 28 that in the church God had appointed individuals to fulfill a variety of functions. The fact that God had designated them to these certain functions should not go unnoticed. God reserves the right to determine what role he gives each of us to exercise. This tells me that my function in the body is not something I decide for myself. God appoints me for my role. This removes any need for someone to seek after those gifts that are showy or that are perceived to be more important than the others. It also challenges us to be content with what God has given us.

The various offices or roles in the church that Paul spoke of here were apostles, prophets, teachers, those working miracles and healing, and those exercising gifts of helps, administration, and tongues (verse 28). The apostles, as originally chosen by the Lord, were eyewitnesses to the Lord and his teaching. Under the inspiration of the Holy Spirit, the apostles founded the early church and taught with authority the word God had given them. Our faith is solidly anchored on the apostles' doctrine and teaching. Their teaching was authenticated by signs and wonders. They spoke and taught authoritatively as Christ's founders of the church.

In the early church before the New Testament was written, the prophet was empowered to communicate God's heart to his people in particular times and situations. This might have been by means of an inspired application of the revealed word of God to a specific situation. It might also have been a word of encouragement, exhortation, or comfort to the body from the Lord at a specific time of need. Prophecy was to be examined in light of the clear authoritative revelation of the apostles.

The teacher was the expounder of the revealed truth of God. This role was established in the early church to explain the truths of the Word of God in a way that would be understandable to the people. The difference between the prophet and the teacher seems to have been in the function they fulfilled in the body. The teacher was concerned primarily for the general truth of the gospel and its correct interpretation and application in the church. The prophet's word was more pointed and specific. If you sat under a teacher, you would leave with a clearer understanding of what the Scripture was saying and a general application for today. You would have gained great insight. Sitting under a prophetic preacher, however, you would have a very definite sense that the Lord was pointing out a specific sin or speaking directly to a particular need you had been experiencing in your life.

God had also, said Paul, appointed in the church "workers of miracles." God used these individuals to proclaim his sovereignty over nature itself. Through the prayers of these individuals, the impossible seemed to happen. Through these individuals, God confirmed his power and authority. They confirmed by signs and wonders the word spoken by the apostles, prophets, and teachers.

Beyond this, there were those gifted in healing. The focus here was physical, emotional, and spiritual healing. These individuals were particularly burdened to pray for these types of healings. God communicated to them his will in this matter, and they prayed with authority for the healing he directed.

Those who had the gift of helping others (helps) were particularly burdened to help those in need. These individuals were somehow able to see needs and opportunities to meet needs that others seemed to overlook.

Those gifted in administration were able to deal with the many details required to move the body of Christ forward. Whether these were political, financial, or practical in nature, these individuals seemed to excel in administration. The delight of this person was to use their administrative ability for the advancing of the kingdom of God.

Tongues were also listed here in this passage as a gift given to the body of Christ. As we mentioned in the last meditation, there were two types of tongues mentioned in the Scripture. The first was the ability to communicate in known languages the revealed word of God. This appears to have been used by God in the early church for communicating his truth in other languages for the rapid spread of the gospel. The second was the ability to speak in an unknown spiritual language. This second use of tongues was for prayer, exhortation of the body (when interpreted), worship, or personal edification.

Paul concluded this section by asking a series of simple questions. Does everyone have the gifts to be an apostle? Is everyone appointed to be a prophet or teacher or a worker of miracles? Does everyone have the gift of healing, or does everyone speak in tongues or interpret tongues? The answer to these questions was obviously no. Each believer was given a different gift.

God has a specific role for each person to play in the advancing of his kingdom. He gives the gifts he deems necessary. This is why we need each other in the body of Christ. If everyone had all the gifts, we would not need each other. God has created us in such a way that we all have need of each other.

In conclusion, Paul challenged the Corinthians to desire spiritual gifts, especially the greater gifts (see 1 Corinthians 14: 1 as an example). Notice how he challenged them to "eagerly desire" these gifts. It is easy for us to sit back and think that if God wants to give me a gift, he will give it to me. This attitude is contrary to what Paul was teaching here. Paul encouraged the Corinthians as a local church body to eagerly seek the full expression of the spiritual gifts, instead of being envious of certain gifts. It should not matter who was given which gift. It should only matter that God was glorified when all the gifts were expressed in a loving unity. May the Lord use us today to advance his kingdom in a loving, unified way for his glory.

For Consideration:

- Have you ever felt as if your gifts were not important? What does this passage teach us about the need for every gift in the body of Christ?

- What gifts do you see in evidence in your church? Is there someone that you need to encourage in the use of his or her gifts?

- What gifts has God given you?

For Prayer:

- Thank God for the gifts he has placed in your church.

- Ask God to make it clear to you what gifts he has given you and the role he would have you to play in the body of Christ.

- If you do not know what gifts you have received from God, take a moment to pray that the Lord would clearly show you.

23

Love is
Patient and Kind

Read 1 Corinthians 13:1–4

I n chapter 12, Paul had instructed the Corinthians concerning the various gifts God had given to the body of Christ. Each person had a gift from God. All these gifts had one thing in common: they were to be exercised in love. Without love, Paul told the Corinthians, their gifts were like "a clanging cymbal." We can speak truth from our lips, but if that truth is without love, it is an annoying sound to the ears of the listener. Someone might have the gift of prophecy and be able to fathom all mysteries and knowledge, but if that gift was exercised without love, it was of no value.

Paul told the Corinthians that they could even give all they had to the poor and die for someone else, but without love all this sacrifice meant nothing. For Paul, love was the essential ingredient in the use of all spiritual gifts. Verses 4–7 are devoted to explaining what love is.

We would all like to believe that we could find perfect ministries or perfect relationships. But the deepest wounds you and I will ever experience in life will come from those we love most. Since the fall of humanity into sin, there has never been a perfect friendship or marriage or ministry. Adam and Eve experienced a loss of intimacy in their marriage and the agony of the death of a beloved son at the hands of his jealous brother. Jacob's wife Leah bore, throughout her life, the pain of her husband's spurned love. David and Jonathan knew the sorrow of separation from each other because of King Saul's jealousy. David also wept over the rebellion of his son Absalom. The father of the prodigal son grieved because of a strong willed, undisciplined, and reckless child. The disciples felt the betrayal of Judas, a trusted companion of three years. Peter knew the shame of denying his Lord three times. And the list goes on.

Because of sin there is hurt and sorrow involved in every relationship. The question we need to ask ourselves is, how should we behave toward others when there is so much pain involved in ministering to them? The answer, according to Paul, is love. Let's examine in detail what Paul taught here about biblical love.

Love is Patient

"Love," said the apostle, "is patient." The word he used here for *patient* (or *suffers long*, NKJV) is the word *makrothumeo*. This word comes from two Greek words. The first of these words is *macros*, meaning "long in time or distance." The second word is *thumos*, meaning "wrath" or "fierceness." Combined, these two words give us our first definition of love. Love is the ability to persevere a long time under the wrath and fierceness of another. *Makrothumeo* can be translated in a variety of ways. It is the ability to endure the insults and pain inflicted by another. It is the patience of a spouse who, day after day, puts up with a mate's cutting remarks and yet remains true and faithful to the marriage. It is the perseverance of a parent who still reaches out in love to a rebellious son or daughter. It is the love of a friend who is there for another even after having been betrayed. It is the love of a holy God who reached down when we were his enemies. It is the love of a Savior who bore our insults and remained on the cross for our salvation.

Love is the ability to endure the pain inflicted by another and yet remain devoted to the offender's well-being. True love accepts the pain, although it does not delight in the pain. There are certainly times when love might even seek to protect itself, but love remains faithful despite the pain. It will not run away when things get tough. It will not abandon its loved one. Love will willingly suffer for the sake of and even because of the one it loves.

All across our nation, relationships are breaking up because they are not founded on biblical love. The greatest example of this longsuffering love is the person of the Lord Jesus. How often have we let him down or grieved him? How many times have we been unfaithful to him? Despite our rebellion, his love remains true. Nothing will change his love for us. Paul put it this way in Romans 8:38–39: "For I am convinced that neither death nor life, neither angels nor demons, neither the present nor the future, nor any powers, neither height nor depth, nor anything else in all creation, will be able to separate us from the love of God that is in Christ Jesus our Lord."

What a comfort this is! The love of Christ for us is such that nothing will ever separate us from him. Despite our shortcomings and our sin, his love remains certain. He leaves us this example to follow. Love is not the absence of pain and suffering but the willingness to endure pain and suffering for the well-being of one another.

Love is Kind

There is nothing quite as powerful as kindness. Brute force will only serve to encourage retaliation. Angry words will give birth to strife. Shunning silence will foster bitterness and frustration. Kindness, on the other hand, will break down barriers.

Paul told the Corinthians that love is kind. The word he used for *kind* is the Greek word *chresteuomai*. This word means "to show oneself useful" or "to act benevolently." *Chresteuomai* comes from the root *chrestos*, meaning "to be employed or useful." It is important to note here that kindness is an action word. The kindness that Paul spoke about here is much more than an attitude of the heart. You cannot be kind if you are not showing yourself useful to those around you. Kindness, by its very nature, involves work. Kindness sees needs, is moved by those needs, and reaches out to do something about them. It involves sacrifice of time and effort for another.

It is one thing to be kind to those who are kind to you, but it is quite another to be kind to those who have made your life difficult. Notice that Paul spoke of love being kind right after speaking about the longsuffering nature of love. The idea here is that love responds in kindness even when being mistreated. Love sacrifices and reaches out at its own expense, even to those who have been cruel and oppressive. Listen to what Jesus tells us in Luke 6:35–36: "But love your enemies, do good to them, and lend to them without expecting to get anything back. Then your reward will be great, and you will be sons of the Most High, because he is kind to the ungrateful and wicked. Be merciful, just as your Father is merciful."

The apostle John put it this way in 1 John 3:16–18: "This is how we know what love is: Jesus Christ laid down his life for us. And we ought to lay down our lives for our brothers. If anyone has material possessions and sees his brother in need but has no pity on him, how can the love of God be in him? Dear children, let us not love with words or tongue but with actions and in truth." True love expresses kindness by laying down its life. It will not count the cost. It willingly sacrifices its material possessions for another (even an enemy). Biblical love takes as its example the person and work of the Lord Jesus.

I remember when I first met my wife. There was nothing I would not do for her. I remember many acts of affection and devotion. I remember the late nights, the early mornings, and the hours of talking. Nothing was too much. No sacrifice was too great. I was in love. I expressed kindness to her in sacrificial deeds and loving consideration of her needs. I looked for ways to be kind.

As time went by, however, my attention began to shift from my partner to myself. I became less considerate of her needs.

I began wanting to be served. I gradually became frustrated when my wife required something from me. Sacrificing for her no longer had the appeal it once had.

Do you want to see your ministry to those around you refreshed and renewed? Put kindness back into your relationships. Look for ways to reach out in active usefulness, as Christ did. You will be amazed at what this will accomplish. Biblical love has eyes that are open to the needs of others and reaches out to be of practical service. The love of Christ in us finds great delight in ministering kindness in small and large ways to those around us.

For Consideration:

- Have you been responsible for causing pain in the lives of others? Take a moment to list some ways you have caused pain. Confess these things to the Lord, and then go to the person you have offended and seek his or her forgiveness.

- How does this passage help us understand what our response should be toward our rebellious children or toward a friend or spouse who has offended us?

- Take a moment to consider if there are people in your life that you have trouble loving because of something they have done to you. What is your response to them?

- How can you minister kindness to those around you? Commit yourself to putting at least one of these things into practice over the next few days.

- Can you think of times this week when you failed to minister kindness to others? Confess this shortcoming to God. Claim the forgiveness offered you in Scripture.

For Prayer:

- Have you ever been deeply hurt by someone? Confess any bitterness, and ask God to help you love this person with longsuffering love.

- Thank the Lord for his longsuffering love for you despite your sin and rebellion.

- Ask the Lord to reveal to you ways in which you can show kindness today. Be ready to hear him when he prompts you.

- Ask the Lord to forgive you for the times when you failed to actively reach out in kindness. Ask him to help you focus less on yourself and more on others.

24

Love Does Not Envy or Boast

Read 1 Corinthians 13:4

Love Does Not Envy

Have you ever struggled with envy? Let's be honest with ourselves. There is not a week that goes by that we do not look at what someone else has and wish that we had something equally as good. Maybe it's a co-worker whose business seems to be much better than ours. Maybe it's a mother or father who seems to have a much easier time raising their children than we do. Maybe it's a student who never seems to have to work to get the grades we spend hours to get. Maybe it's a fellow believer who has a ministry that we could only dream of having.

The Bible often warns us about envy. Paul spoke of envy in Romans 1:28–29 as being the fruit of a depraved mind. In Galatians 5:18–21 Paul listed envy among the acts of the sinful nature along with witchcraft, hatred, sexual immorality, and drunkenness. Peter pleaded with his readers in 1 Peter 2:1 to rid themselves of all envy. What is so wrong with envy that it is treated with such seriousness in the Scriptures? There are three reasons why we need to deal with envy in our lives.

First, we need to deal with envy because of where it can lead us. Genesis 37:11 tells us that Joseph's brothers envied him because of his close relationship with their father. This led his brothers to consider murdering him. When this failed, they sold him into slavery. Matthew 27:18 tells us that it was out of envy that the Jews had Jesus arrested and delivered over to Pilate to be killed. Envy is a tool in the hands of the enemy. If we allow it to remain unchecked, we give Satan a foothold in our lives. There is no telling where envy can lead.

Second, by its very nature, envy is self-centered. Envy says, "I don't like other people having nicer things than I have." Envy is never happy to take second place. It cares nothing about the needs of others. It hates to see others prosper or succeed. This goes against everything Scripture teaches us about considering others as more important than ourselves.

Third, envy despises the will of God. It cannot accept the ways God blesses others. Envy says, "God, I don't like it when you bless someone else; why couldn't you just give all your blessings to me?" It calls God's purposes into question. It takes a stand against God and his sovereign right to bless and give to his children as he sees fit.

Paul told the Corinthians in verse 4 that love does not envy. Earlier, Paul had reprimanded the Corinthians for being jealous of each other: "You are still worldly. . . since there is jealousy and quarreling among you" (3:3). Whereas envy cannot rejoice in the comfort and prosperity of another, biblical love is happy when others are blessed. If we love others, we will rejoice in their blessing. We will not be asking ourselves, why didn't I get that? Or, why do things always work out for him? Love not only rejoices in the success, prosperity, and comfort of others, it actively seeks it. But envy destroys love. It kills our ability to rejoice with others. Envy causes all of life to be viewed through the lens of competition. Proverbs 14:30 tells us: "Envy rots the bones."

One of the tests of Christian love is how we react to the prosperity of others. Does their success or comfort cause us to become bitter? Do we inwardly desire their blessings for ourselves? Can we rejoice when others succeed in areas in which we have failed? Do we sincerely delight in their honor? There is no envy in true love.

Love Does Not Boast

There are some animal species in which, during the mating ritual, the male will seek to impress the female by some great show of strength or dominance. Sometimes he will parade himself around and try to impress the female by his looks. Human beings are not very different. Good looks, intelligence, and skills seem to be very important in our society. We measure the value of an individual by appearance or ability. We compare ourselves with others and measure our abilities and looks against theirs. If we come out on top or, at least, are equal with others, we feel good about ourselves.

Paul stated here in verse 4 that biblical love is not boastful. What did Paul mean by this, and how does it relate to love? In true love there is no need to boast. Why do we boast or parade ourselves? Is it not so that others will accept us and think highly of us? Boasting is a sign of insecurity. If a product does not sell by itself, it has to be promoted so people will buy it. This is why we boast. We draw attention to our abilities so that others will see us, be impressed, and like us. In Christian love this is unnecessary. Paul encouraged the Corinthians to love others with the love with which they were loved—the perfect love of the Lord Jesus, who had accepted them with all their warts and blemishes.

This is true for us as well. We may not be the most intelligent people. We may wish to get rid of a few extra pounds. In authentic love, however, none of these things matter. Love is unconditional. There is something very comforting about this. If we remember that we are loved with the love Paul spoke of here, we will not feel the need to boast. We are accepted as we are by the most important person in the universe—God

Almighty. We will always be accepted by him no matter how things turn out (see Romans 8:31–39). He loved us when we were at our worst. Like the father of the prodigal son, his arms are stretched out to receive us even when we have wandered from him. His love for the ones who serve him faithfully is no greater than his love for the wanderers. We could be laid up on beds of sickness and never able to serve or speak another word on his behalf, and his love for us would not change. Our great achievements on his behalf will not make him love us more. Our shortcomings will not make him love us less. This is true love. This is true security.

There is another thing about boasting that we need to understand. People who boast are self-centered. They do so with the attitude that they are better than others. Their focus is on themselves. This is foreign to what biblical love means. Real love does not seek to impress. Its focus is not on itself, but others. Love concentrates on edifying and lifting up those it encounters. Real love dies to self. It considers others as being more important than itself. If there is any boasting, it is not in self but in the qualities of Christ.

The Lord Jesus never boasted about himself, although he had something to boast about. He never pointed to himself but to the Father he served (see John 12:49–50). The Lord Jesus was secure in the Father's love, and so he was able to love others well. May the Lord show us how to love as he loved.

For Consideration:

• Consider for a moment when you last experienced envy in your relationship with another. What did this indicate about how you really felt about the person?

• Consider for a moment what it was that attracted you to your husband, wife, or friend. Have any of these things changed over time? How has it affected your relationship with this person?

- When was the last time you boasted about the strengths of Christ? Take a moment to thank the Lord for his wonderful qualities.

For Prayer:

- Take a moment to confess your envy to God. Tell him honestly what you feel and why you feel it. Ask him to give you victory over this sin in your life. The next time you experience envy, reject it as sin and instead rejoice in God's blessing in the life of the individual concerned.

- Ask that Lord to help you take your eyes away from yourself in your relationships.

- Thank him for the unending love he has for you.

25

Love is Not Proud, Rude, or Self-Seeking

Read 1 Corinthians 13:4–5

Love Is Not Proud

Proverbs 16:18 tells us that "pride goes before destruction." This is true in relationships. One sure way to destroy a relationship is to allow yourself to become puffed up and arrogant. Pride is the number one enemy of biblical love.

Paul told the Corinthians that love is not proud. The word for *proud* in the Greek language is the word *phusioo*. Very simply, this word means "to inflate," "to fill with air," or "to make oneself higher than another." What is the relationship between pride and love?

In 1 Corinthians 4:6 Paul warned the Corinthians about letting pride set one person against another in the church: "Now, brothers, I have applied these things to myself and Apollos for your benefit, so that you may learn from us the meaning of the saying, 'Do not go beyond what is written.' Then you will not take pride in one man over against another."

This is the dangerous thing about pride. It has a tendency to elevate itself above others. Pride and arrogance foster competition in a relationship. When people puff themselves up in pride, the result is that they begin to expect others to bow to their wishes. The proud person resents the role of servant. An even more serious problem emerges when both people in a relationship puff themselves up in pride. Neither one will give in, and arguments ensue. Christian love, according to Paul, will not elevate itself above another. It will humble itself and consider the needs of another to be more important than its own.

There is another thing about pride: it often refuses to be corrected. Have you ever met people who could not admit they were wrong? I have sometimes laughed to myself while watching individuals trying to make excuses for their mistakes. This inability to admit wrong is a very serious problem in a relationship. We sometimes puff ourselves up to believe that our judgments are always right. Let's admit it: there are times when we are wrong. Have you ever had to go to a family member or church member and apologize for what you said in anger? Love accepts correction. It is not so puffed up that it can not admit its shortcomings. It will humbly listen to rebuke and willingly make the changes necessary.

A third thing about pride is that it is often incapable of admitting needs. Have you ever offered a hand to an individual who was too proud to accept it? Have you ever given counsel to someone who was too proud to admit a need? It is never easy to be vulnerable. We all want people to think that we are better than we really are. There are things that we are too ashamed to reveal even to those who are closest to us. We fear that they will think less of us. To open ourselves up to others and reveal our needs, struggles, and shortcomings is often very difficult. There are times when we can even hide our weaknesses from ourselves. Only in the context of God's love are people free to reveal their deepest struggles and be vulnerable.

Love is not proud. It does not enter into competition with others. Instead, it reaches out to serve. It does not fear correction. Instead, it accepts the gentle rebuke of others and makes the necessary changes. It is not too proud to admit its needs and weaknesses. Instead, it is willing to receive ministry. Only in the context of the love of the Lord Jesus are we free to be ourselves and offer this blessing to others.

Love Is Not Rude

Have you ever heard the expression that familiarity breeds contempt? What this expression means is that the more familiar we are with someone, the worse we tend to treat them. We have seen in the last couple of meditations that in a biblically loving relationship, there is security and no false pretences. Knowing that I am loved regardless of what happens can lead me, however, to take the liberty to say or do things that I should never do or say. Very often we will go the extra mile for a stranger but will not cross the room for someone we say we love. We flatter and praise our acquaintances but cut down those with whom we are more familiar. When we find ourselves doing this, we are not loving with the love of Christ.

Paul told the Corinthians that love does not behave rudely. The word *rude* is translated in different ways in various translations of the Bible. It means to behave in an unbecoming or improper manner. Some dictionaries define *rude* as a lack of grace and refinement or as being discourteous, abrupt, unpleasant, or forceful.

When we make an effort to show grace, refinement, and courtesy to our guests, what are we saying to them? Are we not telling them that we consider them worthy of our utmost esteem? Rudeness, on the other hand, shows contempt. It says, "You are not worth being treated with grace and refinement." By our courtesy or rudeness, we reveal to others what we think about them. If we are willing to show strangers how much we esteem them by our courtesy and refinement, how much more should we do this for those who are closest to us in our families or in our churches? Love deals with others in a way that supports individual dignity.

How many times do we forget to thank others? How many

times have we lacked grace and refinement in our speech with those who are closest to us? How often have we inflicted our unpleasant moods and attitudes on others, treating them like a garbage dump for all our frustrations and hostilities? Love is not rude. It shows grace and refinement in its dealing with others. It values others too much to inflict cruel words and improper behavior on them.

Rudeness is also characterized by forcefulness and abruptness. We say that people are rude if they seek their own way with no concern for others. Love shows respect. It would rather suffer loss than disregard the feelings and needs of others. Love is considerate. Rudeness says, "I know you are tired and weary, but my needs are more important." Love, on the other hand, chooses to minister to the tiredness and weariness at its own expense. It will willingly suffer loss because it values showing the love of the Lord Jesus. It seeks to minister grace and kindness.

Courtesy is one of those things we seem to lose with time in relationships. When things are new and fresh, we find ourselves always expressing appreciation and thankfulness to others, even for the small things they do for us. As time passes, however, we begin to take these things for granted. This can eventually turn into rudeness. What a beautiful thing it is to see an older couple who has relearned the art of courtesy in marriage. While this should be the norm in any relationship, it has become the exception.

Christian love, said Paul, is not rude. It demonstrates in word and deed how much it values others. One of the measures of love is courtesy. If we want to demonstrate love to someone, we will season our words and actions with grace and refinement that is in Christ.

Love Is Not Self-Seeking

In Leviticus 19:18 the Lord God commanded: "Love your neighbor as yourself." We understand from this commandment that love for self is both natural and good. This is the understanding of the apostle Paul when he wrote in Ephesians 5:29:

"After all, no one ever hated his own body, but he feeds and cares for it, just as Christ does the church."

There is within us all a natural desire to care for ourselves. When we are hungry, we feed ourselves. When we are hurt, we will do everything in our power to relieve the pain. Not only is this true regarding the very basic needs of life but also with its pleasures and luxuries as well. The Lord has given us many good things to enjoy. We have all known the joy and satisfaction of basking in the simple blessings of life. It is the most natural thing in the world to care for ourselves and delight in the good things God has so richly provided for us.

Paul told the Corinthians in verse 5, however, that love is not self-seeking. The love Paul spoke about here is stronger than self-love. It is a love that would willingly lay down its life for another. It is demonstrated best in the person of the Lord Jesus and how he lived his life with more concern for others than for himself.

Earlier Paul had said: "Nobody should seek his own good, but the good of others" (10:24). Paul was not saying that we should never care for our own needs. He meant that we ought to be even more concerned about the needs of others. Think about the decisions you make on an ongoing basis every day. How many of those decisions are based on providing for your own needs? Paul told the Corinthians that authentic love cares more for the needs of other than it does for its own needs. If you truly love others, you will find that your decisions have more to do with them than yourself.

Paul put it this way in Philippians 2:3–5: "Do nothing out of selfish ambition or vain conceit, but in humility consider others better than yourselves. Each of you should look not only to your own interests, but also to the interests of others. Your attitude should be the same as that of Christ Jesus."

Love gives priority to the interests of others. We are not speaking here about an inferiority complex or low self-esteem. While Jesus was on earth, he knew that he was the Son of God. He knew that he was perfect and sinless. He knew that the destiny of humanity hinged on his work. Although Jesus knew his value as a man and as God, he gave up earthly comforts to achieve kingdom purposes. He did nothing out of conceit or personal glory. He looked always to the interests of his heavenly Father. To demonstrate the love of the Lord Jesus, we should willingly make sacrifices for the benefit of those around us.

Listen to what Paul said in Romans 14:14–15: "As one who is in the Lord Jesus, I am fully convinced that no food is unclean in itself. But if anyone regards something as unclean, then for him it is unclean. If your brother is distressed because of what you eat, you are no longer acting in love. Do not by your eating destroy your brother for whom Christ died."

Love willingly puts aside legitimate desires and interests for the sake of another. It willingly turns off the television or puts down the newspaper. It is willing to spend less time at work or less time with friends for the sake of its partner. It will not claim its rights. If Christ was willing to die for those around us, we dare not refuse to sacrifice the petty matters of life for their good.

For Consideration:

• Consider the last time you had a disagreement with someone. What role did pride have in this disagreement? What would have happened if you had swallowed your pride?

• Take a moment to write down several ways in which someone ministers to you. Find time this week to thank this person in a special way.

• Very often the only way our families or friends have of telling how much we love them is by how we treat them in word and deed. What have you been saying to them recently? How can you show more courtesy to those around you?

- Consider for a moment how you spend your personal time and money or how you make your decisions. How much of this is focused on your own personal needs and desires? How much is focused on others?

For Prayer:

- Ask the Lord to help you this week to be willing to listen to the reproof of others. Commit yourself to making the necessary changes in your life.

- Ask the Lord to help you demonstrate his love through your words and actions.

- Ask God to help you balance personal needs and ministry needs.

26

Anger and Record Keeping

Read 1 Corinthians 13:5

Not Easily Angered

S ome years ago I was speaking to an individual who told
me that his marriage was almost perfect. In over fifteen
years of marriage, he and his wife had never once had
a disagreement. I immediately wondered where he had been
those years. Every relationship I know has had its share of
disagreements.

There are many things that can provoke us to anger. Paul
told the Corinthians, however, that love is not easily angered.
The word used here comes from two words in the original
Greek. The first word is *para* meaning "near," "in the vicinity
of," or "beside." The second word is *oxus*, meaning "rapid" or
"quick." When you put these two words together, you get the
word *paroxuno.* The idea in this word is to rapidly come near or
possibly lash out at someone. It is what happens when someone
hits a raw nerve in you. It prompts you to respond in anger or
bitterness and to quickly draw near to them in retaliation.

Paul was not saying that love never gets angry. Love, however, is not quick to become angry. There are times when it is morally correct to get angry. We see several examples of this in the Bible. Consider the example of Paul when he went to Athens: "While Paul was waiting for them in Athens, he was greatly distressed (*paroxuno*) to see that the city was full of idols" (Acts 17:16).

We also see the anger of Jesus when he overturned the tables of the moneychangers in the temple (Luke 19:45). These examples show us that there are times when anger is legitimate. In both of these examples, we see that Paul and Jesus became angry when the principles of righteousness were being trampled on. The dishonoring of God and his Word ought to make us angry.

It is very clear in Scripture that there are times when we will be rightly provoked to anger. Notice, however, that Paul told the Corinthians that love does not seek its own. There is an anger that is self-seeking and has very little, if anything, to do with the glory of God. This is an anger that lashes out because its comfort zone has been infringed on or because it has felt offended or mistreated. In cases like this, Peter challenged his readers to look to the Lord Jesus as their example: "To this you were called, because Christ suffered for you, leaving you an example, that you should follow in his steps. 'He committed no sin, and no deceit was found in his mouth.' When they hurled their insults at him, he did not retaliate; when he suffered, he made no threats. Instead, he entrusted himself to him who judges justly (1 Peter 2:21–23).

Listen to the teaching of Jesus in this regard in Matthew 5:39–44:

> But I tell you, do not resist an evil person. If someone strikes you on the right cheek, turn to him the other also. And if someone wants to sue you and take your tunic, let him have your cloak as well. If someone forces you to go one mile, go with him two miles. Give to the one who asks you, and do not turn away from the

one who wants to borrow from you. You have heard that it was said, "Love your neighbor and hate your enemy." But I tell you: Love your enemies and pray for those who persecute you.

Love will not retaliate when insulted. It will absorb offenses and surrender its comforts when called to do so. When compelled to walk one mile, the love of Christ in us will offer to walk a second mile. It will love even those who persecute and make life miserable. Because biblical love does not seek its own, it will not be easily provoked to anger when called on to surrender its rights and conveniences. The supreme example is the person of Christ who surrendered all for us when we were his enemies.

Love Keeps No Record of Wrongs

In any relationship there will be friction and struggle. Few indeed are the relationships where an apology is not required. There are times when we do hurt those we seek to love. These hurts are sometimes difficult to forget. We remind each other of them in very subtle ways. It can come out in subconscious bitterness and rejection or in angry outbursts. At other times, when we are accused, we throw past failures at our accuser to get even.

One of the most wonderful things about being forgiven by the Lord Jesus is that he will never bring a forgiven sin against us. Listen to some of the tremendous promises in Scripture:

- For I will forgive their wickedness and will remember their sins no more. (Jeremiah 31:34)

- As far as the east is from the west, so far has he removed our transgressions from us. (Psalm 103:12)

- You will again have compassion on us; you will tread our sins underfoot and hurl all our iniquities into the depths of the sea. (Micah 7:19)

When we forgive a person, we are in effect hurling their

iniquities into the depth of the sea (Micah 7:19) never to bring them up against them again. We commit ourselves to never make them pay for what they have done to us. We will treat them as if they had never sinned against us.

Paul told the Corinthians that love does not keep a record of wrongs. The word used here is *logizomai*, which has the idea of taking inventory or counting. The love of God in us will not keep track of all the wrongs suffered.

It has been said that love is blind. Love, however, is not naive. It sees the shortcomings of others. It knows that people are less than perfect. It has felt the sting of cutting remarks and rejection. It has suffered through bad moods and angry outbursts. Love, however, covers each of these hurts with the balm of forgiveness. It buries hurts in the depths of the sea, never to bring them up again. Love thinks the best that the case allows instead of assigning evil motives to the actions of others.

The love of God will do its utmost to seek reconciliation so that the enemy does not gain a foothold. Paul stated in Ephesians 4:26–27: "'In your anger do not sin': Do not let the sun go down while you are still angry, and do not give the devil a foothold." The enemy delights in an unforgiving spirit. This is fertile soil for his efforts. When we have unresolved bitterness and anger in our lives, we are very susceptible to Satan's temptations. How many times have we allowed the offenses and insults of others to germinate in our hearts and grow up into a forest of resentment? These little roots of bitterness need to be dealt with immediately: "See to it that no one misses the grace of God and that no bitter root grows up to cause trouble and defile many" (Hebrews 12:15).

The inability to forgive is a major cause of disunity in the body of Christ and in our other relationships as well. For the sake of harmony in the Lord's church and the progress of the gospel in the world, let the Lord set you free of an unforgiving spirit today. The love of God which he has shed abroad in our hearts will not keep an account of wrongs suffered.

For Consideration:

• Can you recall the last time you were angry with someone? How much of that anger was self-centered? What was the real reason you felt angry or bitter?

• What personal comforts or rights, when threatened, provoke you to anger? What does this meditation teach you about these matters? Are you willing to surrender these matters to the Lord for the progress of the gospel?

• What does your description of others reveal about your ability or inability to forgive?

• Have you been hurt in the past by someone? What are your thoughts toward that person today? Are you thinking evil of him or her? Are you willing to forgive right now?

For Prayer:

• Are you easily angered? Ask God to take control of this anger in your life.

• Thank the Lord for his wonderful forgiveness toward you.

• Ask the Lord to give you grace to forgive and move past those wrongs that have been done to you. Ask him to replace the memories of past offenses with his deep love.

27

Love Does Not Delight in Evil But Rejoices in Truth

Read 1 Corinthians 13:6

Love Does Not Delight in Evil

P aul had been speaking to the Corinthians about love. In verse 6, he told them that love does not rejoice in evil. The word used here for *evil* is the word "*adikia.*" This word comes from two words. The first word is *a*, which, when used in this context, changes what follows to the negative. The second word is *dike*, which refers to justice or right. Putting these two words together, we get the idea of injustice or unrighteousness. What does all of this have to do with love?

We can understand the significance of Paul's statement here in a variety of ways. First, love does not rejoice when others are caught up in evil. I think particularly here of the story of the lost sheep in Matthew 18. While there were ninety-nine safe in the fold, the shepherd went out in search of the one that was lost. His heart grieved for the one sheep that had wandered away. The love of God cannot sit idly by when its loved one is caught up in the snare of evil and sin. It will do its utmost to bring the lost sheep back to the fold where it will be safe and secure.

This is the love and concern of a mother whose child has gotten caught up in drugs. This is the concern of a wife whose husband is being snared by the pursuit of money and possessions. It was the concern of a Savior who was willing to leave the glories of heaven to take on the form of a human servant and die so that we could be set free from the bondage of sin and death. Love will not stand by with indifference and watch others perish at the hands of Satan. It will do everything in its power to rescue them from the jaws of this cruel enemy.

Second, love is grieved when others are treated with injustice. No matter how much someone has pained or provoked love, it finds no secret delight in seeing another wrongfully treated. In the Old Testament, the people of Israel had often turned their backs on God. They had been unfair and unjust in their dealings with each other. They had cheated and reduced their brothers and sisters to slaves in order to increase their own personal wealth. Despite their crimes, God found no delight in seeing them mistreated and abused when foreigners invaded their land. He held these nations accountable for their crimes against his people.

Third, love does not take delight in being the source of evil and injustice toward another. This is a continuation of the theme of our last meditation. Love is not easily provoked. It does not find delight in lashing out in vengeance and retaliation. Have you ever chuckled to yourself and said, "I sure put him in his place!" Have you ever patted yourself on the back and said, "Didn't I tell her so?" Have you ever laughed at those cutting remarks that put another person down? Have you ever joined others in their criticism of someone close to you?

Sometimes we can be very cruel to each other. Sometimes we jokingly criticize those we are supposed to love. Many times these remarks hurt. Biblical love, said Paul, does not rejoice in these evils. Love will pursue and practice only those things that build up and edify others. It will not be offensive and critical.

In summary, when Paul told the Corinthians that love does not delight in evil, he was telling them that if they loved someone, they would be grieved if that person wandered into evil (see 5:1–2). They would do everything in their power to bring that individual back to the safety of the fold. They would not delight when the object of their love was mistreated. Love would not find pleasure in seeking revenge or in focusing on shortcomings.

Love Rejoices in the Truth

Love seems to flourish in the context of truth and openness. Where there is truth in a relationship, there is security. Falsehood breeds suspicion and bitterness. Truth is the ground in which biblical love grows. Falsehood, on the other hand, is the fertile soil in which Satan can do his work.

Paul also told the Corinthians in verse 6 that love rejoices in the truth. The understanding here is that love soaks up truth as a parched land soaks up water. Truth brings joy, refreshment, and renewal to love. Love feeds hungrily on truth. It craves it as lungs crave air. The word for truth is *aletheia*. This word comes from two words. The first part of the word is *a*, which refers to an absence of something. The second part of the word comes from the root *lanthano*, meaning "to lie" or "to hide." The word *aletheia* is the freedom from lies. It is a freedom from hypocrisy.

Paul stated in Romans 12:9 that love is to be "sincere." Without sincerity we live a lie. To be insincere is to put on a mask in order to give the impression that we are one thing when, in reality, we are another.

The love of God in us is not put on like makeup. It penetrates to the very core of our being. It saturates everything we do and say. It is real. We all crave this reality. Relationships flourish in this context. The measure of our sincerity is seen in our actions. As the apostle John stated: "Dear children, let us not love with words or tongue but with actions and in truth" (1 John 3:18).

Biblical love, according to the apostle John, goes beyond

saying, "I love you." Authentic love backs up what it says by what it does. It affects how we live our lives and how we respond to each other. It is evident in how we handle our disagreements and difficulties. The love of Christ in us reaches out in practical ways. It is not the person who says, "I love you," who truly loves, but rather the one who demonstrates love in word and deed.

Truth implies sincerity. Love thrives in an environment of honesty and sincerity. In this sort of relationship, we know where we stand with each other. We are not left guessing. We know that we can count on each other through the good times as well as the bad times. The hard times will still be there. We may still have our disagreements, but we know that, despite our differences, our love for each other will carry us through these times. This sort of love is something that others can depend on.

Truth not only implies sincerity of character, but it also has something to do with communication. If we are truthful in a relationship, we do not find it necessary to hide matters from each other. There are many relationships that are characterized by deceit. This was true in the marriage of Isaac and Rebecca when she encouraged Jacob to deceive Isaac in his old age (see Genesis 27).

Often there is a communication breakdown in relationships. People seek to conceal from each other how they are spending money or what they are doing. How many times have you heard statements like, "Don't tell your father," or "My husband would kill me if he found out"? What do these statements reveal about honesty and truth in these relationships? In biblical love there is no need to hide. If we are acting in love, we will be able to speak honestly to others. We will not feel embarrassed or insecure. We will allow others to communicate their desires and failures without us becoming defensive and critical. The love of God in us invites others to be transparent and honest.

For Consideration:

- Can you ever remember a time when you delighted in mocking someone? What does this tell you about how much you were showing the love of Christ at that time?

- Have you been guilty of hiding things from a partner or friend? Why have you felt it necessary to do so? What does this reveal to you about your relationship? Ask the Lord to help you deal with these matters.

For Prayer:

- Ask the Lord to reveal to you any way in which you have delighted in doing evil in your relationships. Seek his forgiveness and commit yourself to seeking to make the necessary changes in your life.

- Ask the Lord to help you be honest in your relationships with others.

28

Love Protects, Trusts, and Hopes

Read 1 Corinthians 13:7

Looking over the city of Jerusalem, Jesus compared his relationship with his people to a hen with her chicks: "O Jerusalem, Jerusalem, you who kill the prophets and stone those sent to you, how often I have longed to gather your children together, as a hen gathers her chicks under her wings, but you were not willing. Look, your house is left to you desolate" (Matthew 23:37–38).

The picture of the mother hen is beautiful. While the mother is exposed to all the elements, under her wings the chicks are sheltered. They are kept warm and dry despite the rain and cold outside.

Paul told the Corinthians that love protects. The word he used is the word *stego*, which literally means "to be a roof over" or "to cover." It also has the idea of enduring or suffering hardship to protect another. Let's go back for a moment to the picture of the mother hen. In order to protect her chicks, the mother hen has to bear or suffer the elements herself. While her chicks are warm and dry, she is exposed to the full force of the wind and rain. She suffers the cold and wet in order to protect her chicks. She becomes a protection or a roof for them.

A roof protects us from the elements. Without a roof we would be terribly exposed. If you are showing the love of Christ, you will be a roof over others. You will be willing to face the foe head-on for the sake of the ones you love. Love naturally protects the object of its affection.

There are many things from which we need protection. First, there is need of physical protection. This is true in the case of parents' love for their small children. Mothers and fathers will show their love for their children by protecting them from physical harm. They will child-proof their homes to keep their little ones from dangerous objects. Authentic love wants to protect others from physical harm.

Second, love will protect from spiritual harm. The apostle John warned his readers not to allow into their homes anyone who did not preach the gospel (2 John 10). While there are many possible interpretations of this verse, one of these interpretations has to do with protecting the family (whether church family or domestic family) from the evil influences in the world. If we love others, we will be careful to shelter them from the evil influences of the world. We will do our part to help them grow in the image of Christ. The same is true in our friendships or marriages. Love will do its utmost to fend off evil influences that would draw another away from the Lord.

Third, love will protect others from emotional harm, which can come in various forms. We can say things to others that will leave them scarred for life. Biblical love will protect others from this sort of abuse. Love understands the impact of its words and will use them accordingly. When someone is hurt, love comes to the rescue. It bandages the wounds. It reaches out to heal and to build up again. It is encouraging and uplifting.

Love will protect and care for others. It will minister healing when someone is hurt. It never tires of protecting. It will willingly face the foe head-on for the welfare of others.

Love Always Trusts

When we read what Paul said to the Corinthians about love always trusting, we have to wonder what he meant. Not everybody we have shown love to has proven to be worthy of our confidence and trust.

What did Paul mean when he said that love always trusts? Was he saying that love is blind and naive? Is he telling us that if we love someone, we will overlook their faults and believe everything they tell us? Is he telling us that if we cannot trust our children in certain areas of their lives, then we really don't love them? Very obviously Paul was not saying any of these things. Paul was saying that love is always seeking an atmosphere of the most trust and confidence possible in every relationship. This confidence will reveal itself in a variety of ways.

First, love inspires confidence by being faithful to others. Where love reigns in a marriage, neither partner will stoop to sexual unfaithfulness or emotional disloyalty. Love will keep people from giving in to destructive temptations. Love is reliable to the end. Love will persevere through difficulty and pain. It will never abandon its loved one.

Second, love promotes confidence in the one it loves. Love encourages others to reach their potential in what God has gifted them to do. This means that love will stand beside others during times of discouragement and frustrations.

Have you ever stood on the sidelines of a race and watched mothers and fathers encouraging their children to do their best? Often a child runs a race looking over to see the smiling, encouraging face of the mother or father. Love stirs the child to do well. It not only sees the potential of others, but it also cheers them on to become what God intended them to be.

Third, love advances confidence in a relationship through its own honesty and sincerity. Love flourishes in truth and redemption. Love is not negative, cynical, or suspicious. It seeks to believe the best about others. Where there is deception and dishonesty there is no love. Love errs on the side of trusting others too much rather than holding back and finding fault.

Where there is biblical love there is confidence and trust. When I say that I love someone, I am, in reality, saying to them that I promise to be faithful to them, to be there for them, to believe in them, and to communicate the truth to them.

Love Always Hopes

One of the things about language is that it is constantly changing. The word *hope* is very often used in our society to express uncertainty. When I say that I hope to do something, it usually means that I would like to do it but am not quite sure if it is going to be possible. This was not the way Paul was using the word *hope* here in our passage.

The word *elpizo*, which Paul used, means to confidently expect. It comes from the word *elpis*, meaning "to anticipate with pleasure" or "to wait with joy." There is something very confident and certain in this word. Look at the way it is used in a number of other biblical passages:

- In his name the nations will put their hope. (Matthew 12:21)

- If only for this life we have hope in Christ, we are to be pitied more than all men. (1 Corinthians 15:19)

- (And for this we labor and strive), that we have put our hope in the living God, who is the Savior of all men, and especially of those who believe. (1 Timothy 4:10)

- Now faith is being sure of what we hope for and certain of what we do not see. (Hebrews 11:1)

- And if you lend to those from whom you expect repayment, what credit is that to you? Even "sinners" lend to "sinners," expecting to be repaid in full. (Luke 6:34)

- And hope does not disappoint us, because God has poured out his love into our hearts by the Holy Spirit, whom he has given us. (Romans 5:5)

The hope spoken of here is a hope that will never disappoint. It will never let us down. It will always be true. If we want to understand what hope in love means, we need to see it in the context of the person of the Lord Jesus. What is our hope in him? How does knowing him give us hope? What is his hope in and for us?

First, we have every hope and expectation that the Lord Jesus will be faithful to his promises. No matter what life may bring, the Lord Jesus will prove true to his word. When things all around us are dark and we cannot see our way, we can simply close our eyes and leap into the darkness with full confidence that the Lord's arms will be open wide to catch us and to direct us through that darkness. We may not understand, but we have every reason to hope with full assurance that he will always come through for us.

When the Lord God told his people in the Old Testament that he would be their God, he meant it. They could move out in confidence in what he said. They had every hope and expectation that he would be faithful to his promises. They could face their enemies with the absolute conviction that he who promised to be their God would be by their side. He would never leave them. He would never forsake them. No matter what the enemy threw at them, they were never without hope as long as they had the Lord.

Second, the Lord Jesus has great expectations about what he can do in us. He knows the plans he has for us. He knows the way he can use us for his glory and honor. He has chosen, in his sovereign purposes, to use us in the unfolding of his plans for the universe. He has great expectations for us. He knows us better than we know ourselves. He knows the sin in our lives and hearts, and yet he is still willing to use us.

What does all this have to do with our love for each other? There is great confidence and hope in biblical love. When we love each other with the love of God, great hope and unity can flourish in relationships. If I am truly loved, I am also assured that others will support me. If I love others, I will encourage them. I am free to be honest in loving relationships. Although we fail each other as humans, God's love for us and in us will never disappoint us. Our ultimate hope is in God and his unshakeable love for us. When we fail and repent, we can always be fully restored to him. Because we have this hope and confidence in God, we are able to offer this unshakable love to others for the furtherance of the gospel and the spread of the kingdom of God on earth.

For Consideration:

• Have you ever found yourself saying things to others that hurt or wounded them? Can you think of times where, instead of being the protector of others, you have been the attacker? Confess these matters to God and those you have wounded.

• Each of us has things we need protection from. What are some of these things? How can you help protect others from negative influences in their lives?

• Have there been times when you did not come through for others? What can you do to make this right?

For Prayer:

• Take a moment to think about the ways the Lord has protected you. Thank him for this protection in your life.

• Take a moment to ask the Lord to help you be someone that others can believe in and trust. Ask him to show you the areas of your life that you need to deal with in this regard.

• Take a moment to confess your shortcomings to God and to the ones you have disappointed in life.

- Thank the Lord for the hope we have in him. Thank him that he places his Holy Spirit in us to make us trustworthy to do the work he gifts us to do.

29

Love Always Perseveres and Never Fails

Read 1 Corinthians 13:7–13

There are times when we get the idea that love makes everything all right. The fairy tales we heard when we were children told us that everyone lived happily ever after. We are surprised when a relationship turns sour. The fact of the matter, however, is that in this sin-cursed earth, relationships can at times become very bitter.

My mind goes back to the Old Testament to a young wife by the name of Leah. She was married to a great man of God by the name of Jacob. The problem, however, was that Jacob also had another wife whom he loved more than Leah. As you read the story of Leah and Jacob in the book of Genesis, you see a woman who desperately tried to get her husband to love her, but to no avail. Throughout her life Leah would struggle with being an unloved wife (see Genesis 29). Many people feel unloved in their relationships.

Paul told the Corinthians that love perseveres. The Greek word for persevere is *hupomeno*, which literally means "to stay under" or "endure." The idea here is that the person who loves is willing to remain under pain or to not flee from the person who is causing pain. This is not an easy thing for love to do. Consider, for example, the life of our Lord. Listen to what the writer of the book of Hebrews tells us: "Let us fix our eyes on Jesus, the author and perfecter of our faith, who for the joy set before him endured the cross, scorning its shame, and sat down at the right hand of the throne of God" (Hebrews 12:2).

We know that the cross was a horrible experience for the Lord Jesus. Physically, emotionally, and spiritually he wrestled with this deepest struggle of his earthly life. What was it that caused him to endure the shame and awful agony? Was it not his love for us? Listen to what Jesus tells us in Matthew 10:22: "All men will hate you because of me, but he who stands firm to the end will be saved."

Jesus told us that we too can expect to have struggles in this life. Because we belong to him, we will be rejected and mocked. People will hate us because of the Lord Jesus. Out of love for him, however, he asks us to stand firm and endure these insults. Perseverance for the sake of the gospel is a real measure of love for Christ.

Even King Solomon knew that there would be many struggles in relationships. He also knew, however, that authentic love would not bail out when things got difficult. It is impossible to extinguish biblical love: "Many waters cannot quench love; rivers cannot wash it away. If one were to give all the wealth of his house for love, it would be utterly scorned" (Song of Solomon 8:7).

There will be times when love cries out in pain. Love will grieve. There may even be times when we wonder if we will not be crushed as we remain under the load we bear. Moses felt this pain. Listen to what he told God in Numbers 11:14: "I cannot carry all these people by myself; the burden is too heavy for me." Here was a man under a heavy load. Moses served out of love, not only for his people but also for his God. Despite his love for God and his nation, Moses cried out in pain as the obligations of his ministry weighed heavily on him.

Yes, love may cry out in deep pain. The test of love, however, is not found in ease but in trial. It is not the young teen couple who has never experienced difficulty in their relationship who really knows what love is. It is the couple who has persevered through marital strife, rebellious children, conflict of personalities, and a whole host of other difficulties and problems who truly understand love. True love shines in all its brilliance against the black backdrop of pain and difficulty.

I am reminded of a family with a mentally handicapped child that attended a church I also attended. I have never ceased to be amazed at the dedication of those parents to care for and minister to their son. Even after they were retired, their son continued to live with them, requiring tremendous care and attention. When the husband died, the mother looked after and cared for her son by herself. Even as an older woman, the mother didn't complain about the extra work or the things she had never been able to do in life. Her love for her son was a persevering love that suffered much but never gave up.

Love Never Fails

Who among us has never once failed to love others? If we are honest with ourselves, there are countless times when we have acted out of pride or selfishness in our relationships. What did Paul mean here when he wrote that love never fails?

The word used here for *never*, in the original language, means "not at any time" or "never at all." The word *fail* is the Greek word *ekpipto*. This word means "to drop," "to fall away," or "to be driven from one's course." Love, said Paul, will never at any time fall away. It will never at all be driven from its course.

Does this mean, then, that if I fail someone, I have just proven that I do not love them? We know that this is not true. Every day we fail those we love in small and sometimes big ways. We know deep in our hearts, however, that we still love them. It would be more true to say that we fail our loved ones not because we don't love them but because we are not acting in love.

It is one thing to love someone in our emotions but quite another thing to act on that love. All too often we do not put into practice the admonition of the apostle John: "Dear children, let us not love with words or tongue but with actions and in truth" (1 John 3:18).

The principle we need to understand here is that when God's love is being acted out, it will never fail to accomplish its purpose. God's love will never cease seeking the good of others. We fail each other in large part because we are not acting out of the true love of God shed abroad in our hearts by the Spirit.

In 1 Corinthians 13:8 Paul told the Corinthians that prophecy, tongues, and knowledge would cease to exist, but love would never fail. In the larger context of this letter, Paul had been speaking of spiritual gifts. He wanted to remind the Corinthians that while these gifts would one day cease, love would never come to an end. Love will exist in the world to come. This was Paul's way of reminding the Corinthians of the preeminence of love in the exercise of spiritual gifts in the body of Christ.

As we have been examining the various aspects of love, I am sure you have asked yourself a question: How could I ever love like that? The day is coming, if you know the Lord Jesus as your Savior, when you will love like this. Paul used the illustration of a child. When he was a child, he did childish things; but when he became a man, he put away those childish things (verse 11). Here below we know only in part; but when the perfect comes, we will know even as we are known. What was Paul telling the Corinthians here? Was he not telling them that on earth we will indeed struggle to love as God has challenged us to love? While still in the flesh, we will wrestle with our childish, sinful nature. Here below we will only know in part what it means to truly love one another; but the day is coming when all this will change. Because love will never fail (never pass away), it will be with us throughout eternity. There in heaven we will know the fullness of love. There we will be set free from the petty things that keep us from loving. There in heaven we will be delivered from ourselves and set free to love each other even as Jesus loves us today.

What does this tell us? It tells us that if there is one thing worth investing in this life, it is love. It is one of the few things we will be able to take with us to heaven.

Second, be assured that it is the will of the Lord to teach us to love. Love is the fragrance of heaven itself. Love was the motivation behind the Lord's life and death for us. It is the will of the Lord that we know his love and show it to those around us.

Are you struggling with the teaching of this passage about love? Do you feel that this type of love is beyond you? To love like this is not natural. We can only love as Paul teaches us by letting the Lord Jesus live and love through us. Shall he whose desire it is that we experience and show his love to one another throughout all eternity not reveal it to us now? He will indeed.

For Consideration:

* Do you have to persevere under a heavy burden in a relationship today? Would you still love others if you knew that they would never provide you with what you are looking for in your relationships? What does this tell you about your love?

* Examine your relationships. Is there any way in which you are not acting out of love towards those around you?

* Have you ever found yourself questioning the love of God for you? What does this meditation tell you about God's desire for you to experience and know his love in your life? What keeps you from experiencing the fullness of God's love for you?

For Prayer:

* Take a moment to ask the Lord to help you love others even as he loves you.

- Thank the Lord that he is willing to teach you to love.

- Ask God to give you strength to persevere in love in the difficult relationships in your life.

30

Tongues and Prophecy

Read 1 Corinthians 14:1–25

Having reminded the Corinthians to pursue love, Paul then challenged them to "eagerly desire" spiritual gifts (verse 1). This was the second time Paul had made this challenge (see 12:31). This underlines the importance of spiritual gifts in the body.

God has chosen to expand his kingdom through people like you and me. He has given us the spiritual gifts necessary for that to take place. How far would we get with our own natural strength and talents? Without God's gifts we would surely fail. It is for this reason that the apostle Paul encouraged the Corinthians to eagerly desire these gifts.

While all of the gifts of the Spirit are important (chapter 12), Paul focused his attention on the gifts of prophecy and tongues in this section. It would appear that there was a problem with the use of these gifts in the church of Corinth. Paul encouraged the use of these two gifts but wanted the Corinthians to know how to use these gifts more effectively.

Paul began by comparing the gift of tongues with the gift

of prophecy. In verse 2, Paul told the Corinthians that the one who speaks in tongues does not speak to humans but to God. Tongues, according to Paul, can be a way of communicating with God. The Holy Spirit uses the tongue of the person with this gift to offer up prayers to God. He or she becomes an instrument through which the Spirit of God prays on behalf of the kingdom.

Tongues are not, in this case, speaking to other people. In fact, the words spoken are not understood by those who hear them (verse 2). Although the person speaking in tongues speaks divine mysteries, the words are not understood without the gift of interpretation.

Those who prophesied, on the other hand, spoke clearly to people for their strengthening, encouragement, and comfort (verses 3–4). While tongues need interpretation, prophecy is clear and edifying. If tongues are not understood, what is the purpose of the gift? Paul gave two reasons why God gave the gift of tongues to the body.

Personal Edification

Those who speak in tongues edify themselves (verse 4). There is great blessing for the individual who has received the gift of tongues. The Spirit of God is pleased to use his or her tongue to proclaim or intercede on behalf of the mysteries of God. God enables these believers to communicate with him in times when they do not know how to pray. Though these believers often do not understand what they are praying, they know that, in their spirits, they are communicating with God and on his behalf. While Paul personally saw prophecy as a better gift because it edifies the church, he coveted the gift of tongues for every believer (verse 5).

Public Edification

According to Paul, there is another use for the gift of tongues in the body. If tongues are interpreted, they can edify the whole body (verse 5). Left without interpretation, tongues remain mysteries. There is a place for the public speaking of tongues in the presence of an interpreter. To explain more fully the difference between tongues and prophecy, Paul gave the Corinthians some practical examples from real life in verses 6–12.

If visitors came to your church when everyone was speaking in tongues, what benefit would they receive? They would not understand anything that was being said. If, on the other hand, someone had a revelation from God—a prophecy, a word of wisdom, or a word of instruction—visitors would be built up and strengthened by what they heard.

Paul gave a second example in verses 7–8. Unless the sounds of a musical instrument made distinctive notes, the listeners would not understand what was being played. If a military trumpet sounded but its notes were not clear, how would the army know that it was time to get ready for battle?

In the same way, said Paul, unless a person produced language sounds that made sense to the listeners, there was no profit to those who heard those sounds (verses 9–11). The purpose of language is to communicate. In light of these facts, Paul encouraged the believers in Corinth to excel in the gifts that built up the body, namely the gift of prophecy.

Because of the nature of the gift of tongues, the person who spoke in tongues was encouraged to pray for the gift of interpretation (verse 13). In this way, the gift could be used not only for personal edification but also for the greater good of the whole body.

In verse 14 Paul told the Corinthians that when people prayed in tongues their minds were unfruitful. The gift of speaking or praying in tongues does not require that the speakers understand what they are saying. The Holy Spirit takes control of their tongues and speaks through them. While this is a wonderful personal experience, Paul encouraged the Corinthians to engage their minds, especially in the context of public worship.

Paul thanked the Lord in verse 18 that he spoke in tongues more than any of the Corinthians. It is clear from this that Paul not only had the gift but also was often edified in its use. While Paul praised the Lord for this gift, he also believed it was better, in public, to speak five words that were understood by the body than ten thousand in tongues. While an individual may be praising God through the use of tongues, no one else is edified (verse 17). For this reason, we should not be sidetracked in the public use of tongues. Our concern, when we gather as believers, is not only to worship God personally but also to edify the body with our spiritual gifts. In our public gatherings, we are to express those gifts that bring the greatest edification to the body of Christ.

Regarding the spiritual gift of tongues, the church of Corinth had been thinking like children (verse 20). They had discovered this new and wonderful gift. They were fascinated by it and focused their attention on it. The gift of tongues was a showy gift that was being abused in Corinth. The Corinthians needed to mature in their exercise of gifts. Speaking in tongues was not a sign of spiritual maturity and not the most important gift. It was not the answer to the spiritual problems of the Corinthians. They could speak in tongues all they wanted and still not see the world come to Christ. The body of Christ needed all the gifts to be operational if it was to advance the gospel message.

The apostle quoted a passage from Isaiah 28 where the prophet told the people that the day was coming when the Lord would speak to his people through the lips of foreigners, yet they still would not listen. In the Old Testament, the unbelieving Israelites heard foreign tongues spoken to them as a sign of judgment as the Assyrians and then the Babylonians captured their land. In the New Testament, God again used tongues as a sign of cursing to unbelieving Israelites as the Lord turned from them and built a new nation out of believing Jews and Gentiles. In verse 22, Paul told the Corinthians that tongues were a sign for unbelievers. Tongues served no purpose among believers in public worship, whereas clear preaching had great value to believers in public worship. In verse 23 Paul reminded them that if unbelievers came to their worship service and heard them speaking in tongues, the unbelievers would think they were foolish. In what sense then were tongues a sign for the unbeliever? There may be a couple of answers to this.

First, tongues demonstrated the power of the Holy Spirit at work. Even though the unbeliever did not understand what was being said, he or she may have been aware of the power of the Holy Spirit in operation through this gift.

Second, Paul may also have been referring to what sometimes happened when the Spirit of God came on an individual in those days. His coming was at times accompanied by some kind of sign or evidence. We read in the book of Acts that one of those signs was speaking in tongues. Paul was not setting a standard here; he was simply telling the Corinthians that sometimes this gift of tongues was a sign to those who came to Christ indicating the presence of God's Spirit in them. It was also a sign of God's presence and power to those who did not believe.

Paul shifted his attention again to prophecy. He reminded the Corinthians that if unbelievers came into the worship service and heard a clear word of prophecy, they would be spoken to directly by God. This prophecy would judge unbelievers in their sinful ways. The prophecy would also reveal the secrets of their hearts. When this happened, they would know that God was not only present but also personally speaking to them. The result would be that the unbeliever would fall down and worship the Lord God, confessing that God was truly among the Corinthians (verse 24–25).

These verses tell us something about the gift of prophecy. Prophecy is the voice of God speaking out against sin. Through his prophets, God reminds people of their sinful ways and challenges them to return to him.

Notice also that prophecy lays bear the secrets of the heart. Throughout the Bible, the Lord revealed to his prophets the secrets of the human heart. Nathan knew, for example, that David had committed adultery with Bathsheba (2 Samuel 12:7–10).

The prophet is given the ability to see things as God sees.

In summary, Paul reminded the Corinthians that while both prophecy and tongues were spiritual gifts to the body of Christ, prophecy occupied a more important role, at least in public worship and service. Unless tongues were interpreted, they brought no specific edification in public worship. Through the gift of prophecy, however, God spoke specifically and powerfully to the whole body. While both gifts were necessary for the full functioning of the body, the church was challenged here to excel in the use of those gifts that brought greater edification to the body as a whole.

For Consideration:

• What is the difference between tongues and prophecy?

• What purpose does the gift of tongues have?

• What role does prophecy have in the church?

• Is there evidence of balance in the use of spiritual gifts in your church?

For Prayer:

• Thank the Lord for the gifts he has given to the body.

• Thank God for those who have used their spiritual gifts to encourage and strengthen you.

• Ask God to give your church all the gifts necessary for the growth and building up of the body as a whole.

31

Ordered Worship

Read 1 Corinthians 14:26–40

Having described the difference between the gift of tongues and the gift of prophecy, Paul moved on to speak to the Corinthians about their worship services. It appears that worship services were getting out of hand in Corinth. Discipline and order needed to be reestablished. This section of 1 Corinthians gives us an understanding of how the worship service of the early church was structured.

Paul began in verse 26 by giving the Corinthians a general principle to follow in their worship. When they came together, he said, everything should be done for the strengthening of the church. One very important goal in gathering together as believers is to strengthen each other in faith. Does your church service strengthen the body of Christ? If it does not, you should give some serious thought to improving this.

When the New Testament believers gathered, they came prepared to participate in worship and the strengthening of the body. Notice in verse 26 how Paul said "everyone" had a hymn, a word of instruction, a revelation, a tongue, or an interpretation. The word "everyone" is important. The implication here is that everyone had a role to play.

I remember some years ago attending a certain church. The pastor led the service, sang the special music, prayed all the prayers, played his guitar to lead the singing, and preached the message. As I left I felt as though I had spent the last hour simply watching this pastor worship God but had not been given the opportunity to express my own heart. Paul expected the Corinthians each to have something to contribute to the worship of their Lord and Savior. It was in the context of the worship service that many of the gifts of the Spirit would be revealed. Is your worship service structured in such a way that the gifts of the Spirit can be used to their fullest measure?

Because people were coming to worship prepared to share their hearts, the possibility of disorder was great. In order to remedy this, Paul encouraged the leaders to provide a structure that would allow the orderly use of spiritual gifts and, at the same time, eliminate confusion and chaos. Paul spent the rest of the chapter giving leaders some guidelines for ordered worship.

Paul encouraged the use of tongues in the worship service (verse 27). At the same time, however, he realized the need for some guidelines in their use. First, tongues needed to be limited to two or three individuals. It would be easy for the whole service to be dominated by those who spoke in tongues. Paul wanted to see all the gifts functioning in worship, not just the showy gifts. For this reason, Paul encouraged the leadership to limit those speaking publicly in tongues to two or three in a given worship service.

Second, also concerning the use of tongues, Paul encouraged the leadership to see that those who did speak in tongues spoke one at a time. The temptation was obviously for everyone with a tongue to speak simultaneously. This only led to confusion. It should be understood here that Paul was referring to the public use of tongues in verse 27. It was not his intention to limit the quiet and private use of tongues in personal praise and thanksgiving during worship. We will come back to this in a moment.

Seeing that public tongues were given for the edification of the larger body, it was necessary that they be interpreted. If there was no interpreter present, then the speaker was to refrain from the public use of tongues and instead speak it privately to God. Paul did not restrict private speaking in tongues without interpretation. The limitation here was in making that tongue public without an interpretation, thus only creating confusion for the body.

Similar restrictions were placed on the use of prophecy (verses 29–33). Only two or three prophets were to speak in a given worship service. Again, Paul wanted to see the use of as many gifts as possible.

As the prophecies were being spoken, others who had the gift of prophecy were to listen and weigh carefully what was being said (verse 29). None of these prophets was infallible. "The spirits of the prophets are subject to the control of prophets," said Paul (verse 32). In other words, what a prophet spoke needed to be confirmed by other prophets. A lone prophet could be dangerous.

Notice third that Paul wanted the prophets to prophesy one at a time, so that everyone would be instructed and encouraged. If a prophet was speaking and another prophet received a word from the Lord, then the first was to be quiet and allow the second prophet to speak. All of this was simply for creating order within the body of Christ.

Notice here that these prophetic words were not prepared in advance. They seemed to have been spontaneous in nature. Notice as well that these prophetic words were for the instruction and encouragement of the body (verse 31). The prophetic word had a teaching element to it. It instructed people in the path God had for them.

Paul moved from tongues and prophecy to the place of women in Corinthian worship services. It should be noticed here that what Paul said about women was not limited to the church of Corinth. He clearly stated that the instructions he gave here were for all the churches of the saints (verse 33).

Women, according to Paul, were to remain silent in church. They were not to speak but to remain in submission, as the Law required (verse 34). Notice that the reason Paul gave for why women should not speak was the law of God.

Paul was not likely referring to any one law here but to the general teaching regarding the role of men and women. God created woman to be a helpmate for man. This is the very clear teaching of Genesis 2:18. This principle was repeated in the New Testament by Paul when he told the Corinthians that "the head of every woman is man" (11:3). He repeated this same thought in Ephesians 5:23 when he said: "the husband is the head of the wife." God gave the role of headship to men. It may be for this reason that Paul challenged the women to be silent.

It is important that we understand what Paul meant here about women being silent in the church. Did Paul mean that a woman was to maintain absolute silence in the presence of men during worship? This cannot be what Paul meant because he had already given instructions concerning how women were to cover their heads when they prayed or prophesied in worship (11:5). Scripture contains various references to women praying in the temple or in the presence of men (Acts 1:14; 2:18; Luke 2:36–37).

The context indicates that the speaking Paul referred to here had something to do with a woman refusing to be in submission: "They are not allowed to speak, *but must be in submission*" (verse 34). This same connection was made by Paul in 1 Timothy 2:12: "I do not permit a woman to teach *or to have authority over a man*; she must be silent." What Paul seems to have been saying is that the woman was created to be a helpmate to the man. Women were not to take authority in the church by taking the role of preacher and teacher. This was reserved for the spiritual men in the church.

It should be noted that the women of the day were, for the most part, uneducated. Paul encouraged women, if they needed explanation of what was being said, to ask their husbands to explain it to them at home to avoid confusion in worship. According to Paul, it was a disgrace for a woman to speak in the church (verse 35). She needed to accept her role as helpmate and be content to exercise that role without taking authority over men.

Paul concluded this section on orderly worship by stating his authority. He reminded the Corinthians that what he had to tell them came from the Lord. To disregard the principles Paul spoke of here was to incur judgment. God himself would turn his back on the church that ignored this teaching (verse 38).

In conclusion, Paul told the church of Corinth to be eager to prophesy and not to forbid the speaking in tongues. In all this, however, the church was to be careful to do everything in an orderly and fitting manner.

For Consideration:

- Does your church provide opportunities for the use of the various gifts of the body? What gifts are not being used in your church?

- What role do the gifts of tongues and prophecy play in the context of your church? Why do we fear the use of these gifts?

- What outlets for ministry does your church provide for women?

For Prayer:

- Ask God to show you the role you need to play in your church.

- Ask God to open up even greater opportunities in your church for all the gifts he has given to be exercised.

32

He is Risen

Read 1 Corinthians 15:1–34

Tabhere was a false teaching circulating in the area of
Corinth. Some people were saying that there was no
resurrection (verse 12). Paul wanted to set the record
straight. He did not want any confusion on this major Christian
doctrine.

He began by reminding the Corinthians that it was through
the gospel he had preached to them that they had been saved
(verses 1–2). He was also assured that the Corinthians stood
firmly on the truths he had taught them.

Verse 2 causes some difficulty. Paul told the Corinthians
that they would be saved by the gospel that he preached to them
"if they held firmly," otherwise they had believed in vain. What
was Paul telling these believers here? He seems to have been
reminding them that salvation is not simply a commitment to
doctrine. Correct doctrine is important, but it will not save anyone. You may understand the message of the gospel perfectly
in your mind, but if you are not experiencing the reality of it in
your life, it means nothing. There are people who believe that

Jesus died for sins and rose again from the dead who will not be in heaven because they have never truly been saved. Paul told the Corinthians that they must not only believe these words but "hold firmly to them."

If you hold firmly to something, you will never let it go. You will not be distracted from it. Paul was telling the Corinthians that this was the test of a true believer. The true believer not only believes in the doctrine of Christ and his work but also holds firmly to it as the only hope for salvation. Authentic believers will not be tempted by modern philosophies. Their eyes will be fixed firmly on their Lord and Savior alone. They will place all their confidence on him. They will live and die for the truth they believe.

There are others whose faith consists only of a set of doctrines. Their faith is not a faith that perseveres. As in the parable of the sower, some seeds fell among the thorns (Matthew 13:3–8). The cares and concerns of this life choke them, and they do not grow into mature plants. These people believe in vain. They know all the right doctrine, but they do not live that doctrine. It is in their heads but has never reached their hearts and souls.

True believers not only believe the words of the gospel but also hold firmly to these words to the end. They will live and die for these words. Paul was not teaching that believers can lose their salvation here. He was rather teaching how to distinguish a true believer from a counterfeit believer.

Having made this distinction, Paul moved on to discuss with the Corinthians what the message of the gospel really is. The gospel, according to Paul, consists of three principal points. First, Jesus Christ died for our sins according to the Scriptures. His coming was foretold by the prophets of old. He was sent from God to this earth to die as a sacrifice on our behalf (verse 3).

Second, Jesus was buried (verse 4). His death was very real. There were those who tried to say that Jesus did not really die. Paul wanted to make it clear that Jesus went all the way for our sins. If Jesus did not die, the penalty for our sins would not have been paid. The law of God stated that the penalty for sin is death (Romans 6:23; Ezekiel 18:4). Jesus truly did die for our sins. His burial was proof of his death.

Third, Jesus rose from the dead (verse 4). Death could not keep him in the grave. He was victorious over sin, death, and hell. Because of this he is our assurance of victory.

Paul went on to tell the Corinthians that this resurrection was witnessed by a number of people (verses 5–8). The risen Christ appeared to Peter and the twelve disciples. Later on, he appeared to over five hundred people. We are not told when the five hundred saw Jesus, but at the time of Paul's writing, many of these individuals were still alive. Later on Jesus appeared again to James and the apostles and finally to Paul himself (probably on the road to Damascus).

Paul was saying that there were plenty of people who witnessed the resurrection of the Lord Jesus. The fact of the resurrection was certain. There could be no doubting that Jesus was alive and had conquered death and hell.

Paul himself was an eyewitness to the resurrection of the Lord Jesus, although he felt unworthy of this honor. In verse 9 he reminded his readers that he was the least of all the apostles because he had persecuted the church. He knew that, after all he had done against Christians, he did not deserve to be forgiven and given the ministry of an apostle. By the grace of God, however, Paul had become a believer and a strong servant of the Lord. That grace of God worked in him, giving him a passion for the lost. God had become so real to Paul that he worked and served him more than all the other apostles (verse 10).

In the verses that follow, Paul reminded the Corinthians how important it is to believe in the resurrection of Christ. Some believed that there was no resurrection (verse 12). To Paul, this was foolishness. How could anyone say that there was no resurrection when Christ's resurrection was clearly witnessed by hundreds of people?

In verses 14–19 Paul reminded the Corinthians of just how

futile things would be if Jesus had not risen from the dead. First, Paul reminded the Corinthians that if Christ was not raised, then Paul's preaching and faith were in vain (verse 14). The gospel of salvation he preached was solidly anchored in the resurrection. If Christ was not raised from the dead, then what Paul preached was useless, and he risked his life for nothing.

Second, if Christ was not raised, the witnesses had lied (verse 15). If the resurrection was not true, then Paul and others had been deceiving those who had heard them preach. The apostles and others were liars and deceivers. If Christ was not raised, the witnesses were offering a false hope to a dying world.

Third, according to Paul, if Christ was not raised, the Christian faith is futile, and those who have gone before us are lost eternally (verse 15). What purpose would it serve to be a Christian if our God was not victorious over sin and death? Could we serve a God who could not overcome sin and death? What hope would there be for our eternity if the Lord Jesus himself could not overcome death and the grave? If Christ did not conquer the grave, then there can be no hope of anything beyond this world.

If there was no resurrection, Christians were to be pitied above all people (verse 19). They were risking their lives for a false hope. They were serving a God who could never save them. For Paul, the truth about the resurrection was essential. It was the central hope of the believer.

In verses 30–32 Paul reminded the Corinthians of how futile his own ministry would be if there was no resurrection. Why would he endanger his life preaching a gospel if it was not true? Every day he had to die to himself to serve the Lord Jesus. In Ephesus, he fought wild beasts because of his stand for the gospel. Why would he do these things if Jesus was not raised from the dead? All his efforts would be fruitless and vain. We are not told what sort of "wild beasts" Paul had to face in Ephesus. Some believe that Paul had been thrown to the wild beasts in an arena and survived. Others see him speaking symbolically about the wicked people in Ephesus who opposed the gospel.

Having reminded the Corinthians of the futility of their faith if there was no resurrection, Paul proceeded to reassure his readers that the Lord had risen and their hope was not in vain. Christ is the firstfruits from the dead, Paul told his readers in verse 20. The firstfruits from the garden were presented to the Lord as a thanksgiving (see Exodus 23:16; Deuteronomy 26). This first of the crops was a promise of more to come. As Jesus was the first to be raised from the dead, he is the promise of more resurrections to come. Adam brought death to the whole world, but Jesus brought resurrection from death to those who believe in him (verses 21–22). When the Lord Jesus returns, there will be other resurrections (verse 23).

According to Paul, the Lord Jesus will destroy all other dominion, authority, and power (verse 24). Christ will return to earth to conquer and destroy all the enemies of God. The last enemy to be destroyed will be death itself (verse 26). God the Father has given to Christ this authority. After he has conquered all, the Lord Jesus will turn everything over to his Father (verse 28). We serve a living and conquering Lord.

In Corinth there were those who were being baptized on behalf of their departed loved ones, with the hope that this baptism would impart some favor to them in the afterlife. Nowhere in Scripture is this commanded for believers. Paul was not encouraging this type of baptism. He was merely using this as an illustration to prove a point about the resurrection. When Paul was in Athens, he used an idol dedicated to an unknown God to share the message of the gospel with the people of Athens (see Acts 17). In using this idol as a witnessing tool, Paul was not condoning the practice of idolatry. He was merely using a cultural practice to illustrate the gospel. In our passage Paul seems to have been doing the same thing. He reminded the people of this pagan practice. Why would anyone practice a baptism for the dead, said Paul, if there was no resurrection from the dead? Even the pagans of Corinth believed in a resurrection.

In this section of Scripture, Paul reminded the Corinthians just how important it was for them to hold tightly to the doctrine of the resurrection of Jesus Christ. Without this doctrine they had no hope. Their preaching would be futile, and their lives and sufferings for the gospel would be in vain (verses 30–33). If Christ did not rise from the dead, they could live only for the present and perish in their sins. The Corinthians needed to be careful who they kept company with. Keeping company with those who did not believe in the resurrection was spiritually dangerous. Paul pleaded for the Corinthians to live soberly in the truth they knew and share that truth with others who were ignorant about the truths of God (verse 34).

For Consideration:

- What does this chapter teach us about the importance of the doctrine of the resurrection of Jesus?

- What does Paul teach us here about what it means to be a true believer?

- Could it be said that many times we do not live our lives in light of the fact that the Lord Jesus is alive and returning one day to this earth?

- If we really believe in the resurrection from the dead, what impact will this have on how we live our lives here below?

For Prayer:

- Thank the Lord that he has conquered death.

- Ask God to help you to live your life with the understanding that he has risen to offer you new life and hope. Ask him to set you free from the futility of living only for this world.

33

What Happens to the Dead?

Read 1 Corinthians 15:35–58

Paul's discussion about the resurrection brought up some practical issues. If there was a resurrection, as Paul claimed, how would the dead be raised? What would the resurrected body be like? Paul addressed these particular questions in this next section.

To answer these questions, Paul began by sharing with the Corinthians an example from the world of plants. When a seed is put in the ground, he told the Corinthians, it is necessary that the seed dies in order that a plant might grow from it. When small seeds are planted in the garden, the expectation is that those small seeds will produce larger plants that, in turn, will produce fruit. The seed does not at all resemble the fully matured plant. In a very similar way, when this earthly body dies and is planted in the ground, we can expect that when it is raised to life again, it will be very different from the body we presently have.

Not all flesh is the same (verse 39). Even in the animal kingdom, there are many different types of bodies. Birds have one type of body and fish have another. Their bodies have very different characteristics for different purposes. God has created different earthly bodies suitable for different kinds of earthly existence.

In the same way, there is a difference between earthly bodies and heavenly bodies (verses 40–41). Just as the sun and the moon differ in splendor, so will our earthly body differ from our heavenly body. We should not expect that we will go to heaven with these present bodies. God is able to create a type of body suitable for resurrection life. In what way will our new heavenly body differ from this earthly body? Paul described some of the differences for his readers.

First, the new body will be imperishable (verse 42). We all know how fragile life is here on this earth. At best, we might live eighty or ninety years, then we die. Many things can shorten those years of our life. Sickness, tragedy, or violence can snuff out our lives in an instant. This will not be the case with our new bodies. They will never die. Sickness will not harm them. Old age will never weaken them.

Second, the new body will be glorious (verse 43). The present body we now have is a marvel of creation. The abilities I have to see, hear, and speak are wonderful. This body reflects something of the glory and majesty of the Creator. On the other hand, however, this body deteriorates and is capable of the worst forms of crimes imaginable. My heart can be deceitful and corrupt beyond measure. My mouth can utter profane and hurtful words. The effects of sin have devastated this marvel of creation.

All this corruption will be reversed in the age to come. The new body will be glorious. It will reflect the glory of the one who created it in a way that it presently cannot. It will be unaffected by sin and its consequences. In the heavenly body, I will no longer wrestle with my sinful ways and temptations. My lusts and evil desires will be no more. No longer will evil and corrupt words be heard from my lips. This new body will be glorious. It will be a clear reflection of Christ.

Third, the new body will be powerful (verse 43). In this present body, I am limited. In reality, as wonderful as the earthly body is, it is very weak and helpless. Tiny insects are able to carry objects many times their own weight. This is not true of the human body. I have never ceased to be amazed at how tiny animals are able to find a hole in a tree or in the ground somewhere and survive through even the coldest of winters. The human body is incapable of doing this. As we have already said, this human body is prone to becoming tired, weak, and sick. While my heavenly body will not be all-powerful (God alone is all-powerful), it will be a strong and healthy body unlike anything I have experienced here below.

Fourth, the new body will be spiritual (verse 44). It will be a body that is in tune with God and his eternal plans. It will be a body that is designed for eternal communion with God and the enjoyment of God unhindered by the sinful nature we now have. We should not understand from this, however, that we will have no physical form. The Lord Jesus, when he rose from the dead, had a physical body that the disciples could both touch and recognize (Luke 24:39).

We received our earthly bodies through Adam, the first man, as we are all his descendants. Our new bodies, however, will come through Christ. Paul reminded the Corinthians in verse 48 that "as is the man from heaven, so also are those who are of heaven." Even as we are presently like Adam, we will one day be like Christ (verse 49).

Paul reminded his readers in verse 50 that "flesh and blood" cannot inherit the kingdom of God. When Paul spoke here about flesh and blood, he was referring to the earthly human body. He was not saying that we will not have a body like the resurrected Jesus. He was simply saying that this present body of flesh and blood will not go with us to heaven. This body we will shed with all its sin and imperfections. We will take an imperishable and sinless body with us to heaven. Even those who do not die before the Lord returns will need to shed this present body of flesh and blood before entering heaven (verse 51).

When will all this happen, and how will it happen? Paul reminded the Corinthians that this whole process was a mystery. No mere human can ever understand the mind of God. This process of raising the dead and giving them a new body is beyond our ability to understand.

Paul did know, however, that this process would be an instantaneous one. In other words, we will be changed in the twinkling of an eye (verse 52). In the time it takes for you to blink, you will receive a new body. What a powerful God we serve. Nothing is impossible to him.

When will this process take place? Paul reminded the Corinthians that this change would take place at the last trumpet (verse 52). That trumpet will sound when God raises the dead on the last day. On that day we will all be given our imperishable bodies. This seems to imply that believers, whose physical bodies are in the grave, have not yet received their resurrection bodies, although their souls have gone to be with the Lord. On the day when the Lord God transforms dead bodies into resurrection bodies and swallows up death in victory, heavenly souls will be clothed in their resurrection bodies (verse 54).

What happens to the old body? As we know, the physical body simply decomposes in the grave. We will never see that body again. The body we will see is a completely new, spiritual body. If our old earthly bodies are not taken with us to heaven, how are we to understand the resurrection of the dead? God will raise up from the grave a new body that will be joined together with our soul. Even as he raised up Adam from the dust of the ground on the day of creation, so again he will raise up a new body for each believer from the grave. That new body will be made out of imperishable elements. It will never die. Sin caused the old body to die, as this was the result of the curse on Adam (see Genesis 3:19). That curse only has an effect on the earthly body. But through the work of the Lord Jesus, the curse will end one day. He gives us the victory (verse 57). Because he has dealt with sin, death's sting has been destroyed.

In light of these truths, we ought to stand firm (verse 58).

Nothing should move us from our commitment to Christ and his kingdom. Nothing should distract us from our labors. We know that our efforts will not be in vain. Our hope is secure. The worst that this world can do to us is take the perishable body we will one day shed anyway. Our hope is not in this life. It is in the life to come.

For Consideration:

• What limitations do we have in our present bodies? What promises does Paul give us here concerning our new bodies?

• How should the understanding of the resurrection influence how we live for and serve the Lord here below?

For Prayer:

• Thank the Lord for the precious promises he gives us here in this section of Scripture.

• Ask God to help you to place your priorities on things above and not on the temporary things of this earth.

34

Concluding Comments

Read 1 Corinthians 16

Paul concluded his letter to the Corinthians here with a series of comments on various subjects. We will examine these individually.

Collection for Jerusalem (verses 1–4)

Paul began with some comments about an offering that the Corinthians were collecting for the church in Jerusalem. Both the Corinthian and Galatian believers were collecting money to ease the burden of poverty among believers in Jerusalem. Paul encouraged the Corinthians to put money aside each Sunday when they met. Some people could give more than others, but each person was to contribute what they could. Paul planned to visit the Corinthians, and he wanted the collection process to be completed prior to his arrival. Paul would write letters of introduction for certain men to take this money to the church in Jerusalem. According to verse 4, he was also willing to accompany them on this journey.

What is important for us to note here is that the apostle

capital city. Aquila, Priscilla, and the church that met in their home sent their greetings. Paul had met this couple originally in Corinth (Acts 18:1). Aquila and Priscilla had become very involved in the work of ministry.

Paul encouraged the believers to greet each other with a holy kiss. This appears to have been the standard way for Christians to greet at this time.

Final Word (verses 21–24)

Paul concluded by telling the Corinthians that he wrote this part of the letter in his own handwriting. Paul's letters were usually dictated to a scribe, but sometimes he hand-wrote a greeting to authenticate the letter and also to make it more personal. Some commentators believe that this was because he had poor eyesight.

Paul called a curse on anyone who did not love the Lord. We should not see this as being a curse on all unbelievers. Paul may have brought this curse on those who called themselves believers but did not live in the love of Christ. These individuals were blemishes on the church and blasphemed the name of the Lord by their hypocritical lives.

In verse 22 Paul used the Aramaic expression *Maranatha*, meaning, "Our Lord, come!" This may have been a common greeting in the early church. This reminded the Corinthians that the Lord was coming again. They needed to live their lives in light of his return. Paul concluded by reassuring them of his deep love for them and wishing God's grace for them, as he had begun this letter (1:3). After all the things we have seen happening in the church of Corinth, they truly did need to be reassured of God's unmerited favor that is the essence of the gospel of Christ.

For Consideration:

• Is your church involved in missionary projects, as were the churches of Corinth and Galatia?

- What does this chapter teach us about the need of discipleship in the body of Christ?

- Examine Paul's attitude in this chapter toward the Corinthians. What does this tell us about the attitude we need to have toward those who are still immature in the faith?

For Prayer:

- Take a moment to consider the needs of other churches in your area. Ask God to meet these particular needs.

- Take a moment to pray for a Christian who is weak in the faith. Ask God if there is anything he would have you do to help this person mature spiritually.